THE TRAIL OF BLOOD

Following the Christians Down Through the Centuries
or
The History of Baptist Churches
From the Time of Christ, Their Founder, to the Present Day

by Dr. J. M. Carroll

(PD) THIS BOOK IS IN THE PUBLIC DOMAIN

ISBN: 978-1-365-48945-7

Published by:
School of Biblical & Theological Studies
www.bibleschool.edu

THIS LITTLE BOOK is sent forth for the purpose of making known the *little-known* history of those FAITHFUL WITNESSES of the Lord Jesus, who, as members of the CHURCH JESUS BUILT, **"Overcame Satan by the blood of the Lamb, and by the word of their testimony: and they loved not their lives unto death,"** (Revelation. 12:11).

I'd appreciate hearing from you--and may I ask your help in getting these messages to our young people and others. Tell them about the wonderful facts of history brought out in this book. Urge them to order it. It would be most helpful to study it in Sunday School classes, Training Unions, Bible Institutes, and other organizations.

TABLE OF CONTENTS

INTRODUCTION (by Pastor Edward R. DeVries, Th.D.)............5

THE TRAIL OF BLOOD (by Dr. J.M. Carroll)

    LECTURE ONE..9
    LECTURE TWO..23
    LECTURE THREE..33
    LECTURE FOUR..41
    LECTURE FIVE..49

    SOME AFTER WORDS...61

    PARTIAL BIBLIOGRAPHY..65

    CHART..67

INTRODUCTION
By Pastor Edward R. DeVries, Th.D.

Recently I took a small group on a trip to Washington, Texas, the birthplace of the Republic of Texas. We went to Independence Hall, and to the Republic of Texas museum. We passed a nearby Baptist Church and we stopped in. The church is just as it was in the 19th century with the oil burning chandeliers, pump organ, and bench-style pews (one of which Sam Houston carved his initials in). I was allowed to examine the records. The church was organized in 1839 and is the oldest Baptist church in Texas. In 1854 Sam Houston was converted in the church and baptized in the nearby creek by her pastor, Rufus Burleson (who also served as President of Baylor University). I was privileged to preach from the church's old pulpit. B.H. and J.M. Carroll, George W. Truett, J. Frank Norris, Jack Hyles, Lester Roloff, and anybody who was anybody in the history of Texas Baptists have preached from that same pulpit.

Dr. J.M. Carroll was ordained by Independence Baptist Church in that same little chapel.

I asked the church secretary, who was conducting our tour, if she had ever read Dr. Carroll's book The Trail of Blood? She had never heard of the book. In the church bookstore there were other books for sale on the History of Baptists written by modernist Southern Baptist seminary professors outlining new revised Baptist history. I call it revised history because it is similar to what the liberal educational establishment is doing in re-writing history in our public school textbooks. (For example did you know that it was now a woman and not Paul Revere who made the famous midnight ride?) The liberals who have taken over Baptist institutions of Education have been engaged in an effort to re-write the history of our rich heritage of faith. According to the new version of Baptist History, the Baptist faith is a Protestant denomination that began in Europe during the Reformation.

Sadly, the members of this historic church have embraced the revisionist history having never even been taught the true origins of our New Testament Baptist faith. Saddened by the fact that in the very church that produced the great man of God, Dr. J.M. Carroll, there were none left who had read his great book. I set out to obtain a copy for the church's library only to discover that the Ashland Avenue Baptist Church in Kentucky, where Dr. Carroll had Pastored, and which had been printing the book, has now ceased production. Dr. Carroll never sought a copyright for his lectures, and even if he had, they were given so long ago that any copyright would have long ago expired. So I decided to bring the book back into print.

ABOUT DR. CARROLL

Dr. Carroll was born in Arkansas, January 8, 1858. He was one of two preacher sons of a preacher father. His brother Benejah Harvey also became a leader among Texas Baptists and founded Southwestern Theological Seminary. The influence of this one Arkansan family upon Texas Anabaptism and Landmarkism around the world cannot be measured. There he was converted, baptized, and ordained to the Gospel ministry. Dr. Carroll not only became a leader among Texas Baptists, but an outstanding figure of Southern Baptists, and of the world.

As a Historian Dr. J.M. Carroll was without question the preeminent scholar on Church history and the Faith of our fathers during the guilded age of the turning from the nineteenth to the twentieth century. It was a difficult time for Anabaptism in America. Fundamentalism was warring against "the new enlightenment" while Liberalism was eating away at the heart of the Bible Belt. Men like J.R. Graves, the brothers Carroll, and later J. Frank Norris, and Ben M. Bogard, were badly needed to remind our fathers of where they had come from. And how long their Faith had endured through much harder times than these under the cruelest of persecutions.

Dr. J.M. Carroll traveled across Texas and other parts of the country confirming Baptists in their most holy faith and recalling for them their heritage. A man by the name of Dr. J. W. Porter attended the lectures and requested the manuscripts that he might publish a book. Dr. Carroll fulfilled the request for a written version of the lectures for the work of publication including the chart he used in the lectures. Then Dr. Carroll died on January

10, 1931, never holding a copy of this book in his hands. It had yet to come off the press. But thanks to Brother Porter the lectures of Dr. J.M. Carroll are here preserved to tell the tale of our beloved and venerated sires in the Faith. From the time that Christ did author and finish it until the rising up of criers in the night to recall the Old Landmarks of the Once delivered Faith of God. And here they are as only a scop of Carroll's class could tell them. The stories of the Earnest Contenders for that self-same Once Delivered Faith and of that simple form of Church founded upon the Rock of Ages.

Perhaps the greatest work of our dearly beloved Brother Carroll was his simple list of marks of the New Testament Church. By the which he tried the brethren of the past to determine who were the children of the apostles in faith and verity, and thus the fathers of ourselves in the same. And these may also be applied by us and all to determine if our Churches are now of Christ and if our Faith be His. And so for the legacy of the Carroll family we now bow our knees to Father of our Lord Jesus Christ, for whom the whole family in Heaven and Earth is named and pray to the Revealer of Hearts that he would guide us in our most holy quest to find the heir apparents who have received like and precious faith to that of old. Or simply stated, to find who are the New Testament Churches in our own century.

"MARKS OF THE NEW TESTAMENT CHURCH"

Its Head and Founder--CHRIST. He is the law-giver; the Church is only the executive. (Matt. 16:18; Col. 1:18)

Its only rule of faith & practice--THE BIBLE. (II Tim. 3:15-17)

Its name--"CHURCH," "CHURCHES." (Matt. 16:18; Rev. 22:16)

Its polity--CONGREGATIONAL--all members equal. (Matt. 20:24-28; Matt. 23:5-12)

Its members--only saved people. (Eph. 2:21; I Peter 2:5)

Its ordinances--BELIEVERS' BAPTISM, FOLLOWED BY THE LORD'S SUPPER. (Matt. 28:19-20)

Its officers--PASTORS AND DEACONS. (I Tim. 3:1-16)

Its work--getting folks saved, baptizing them (with a baptism that meets all the requirements of God's Word), teaching them ("to observe all things whatsoever I have commanded you"). (Matt. 28:16-20)

Its financial plan--"Even so (TITHES and OFFERINGS) hath the Lord ordained that they which preach the gospel should live of the gospel," (I Cor. 9:14)

Its weapons of warfare--spiritual, not carnal. (II Cor. 10:4; Eph. 6:10-20)

Its independence--separation of Church and State. (Matt. 22:21)

"THE TRAIL OF BLOOD"

or

Following the Christians Down Through the Centuries
From The Days of Christ to the Present Time

Or to express it differently, but still expressively:

"A history of the Doctrines as taught by Christ, and His Apostles and those who have been loyal to them."

FIRST LECTURE

"Remember the days of old. Consider the years of many generations; Ask thy father and he will show thee. Thy elders and they will tell thee" (Deuteronomy 32:7).

1. What we know today as "Christianity" or the Christian Religion, began with Christ, A.D. 25-30 in the days and within the bounds of the Roman Empire. One of the greatest empires the world has ever known in all its history.

2. This Empire at that period embraced nearly all of the then known inhabited world. Tiberius Caesar was its Emperor.

3. In its religion, the Roman Empire, at that time, was pagan. A religion of many gods. Some material and some imaginary. There were many devout believers and worshipers. It was a religion not simply of the people, but of the empire. It was an **established** religion. Established by law and supported by the government. (Mosheim, Vol. 1, Chap. 1.)

4. The Jewish people, at that period, no longer a separate nation, were scattered throughout the Roman Empire. They yet had their temple in Jerusalem, and the Jews yet went there to worship, and they were yet jealous of their religion. But it, like the pagan, had long since drifted into formalism and had lost its power. (Mosheim, Vol. 1, Chap. 2.)

5. The religion of Christ being a religion not of this world, its founder gave it no earthly head and no temporal power. It sought no establishment, no state or governmental support. It sought no dethronement of Caesar. Said its author, "Render unto Caesar the things that are Caesar's and to God the things that are God's." (Matt, 22:19-22; Mark 12:17; Luke 20:20). Being a spiritual religion it was a rival of no earthly government. Its adherents, however, were taught to respect all civil law and government. (Rom. 13:1-7; Titus 3:1; 1 Pet. 2:13-16)

6. I want now to call your attention to some of the landmarks, or ear-marks of this religion--the Christian Religion. If you and I are to trace it down through 20 long centuries, and especially down through 1,200 years of midnight darkness, darkened by rivers and seas of martyr blood, then we will need to know well these marks. They will be many times terribly disfigured. But there will always be some indelible mark. But let us carefully and prayerfully beware. We will encounter many shams and make-believes. If possible, the very elect will be betrayed and deceived. We want, if possible, to trace it down through credible history, but more especially through the unerring, infallible, words and marks of Divine truth.

Some Unerring, Infallible Marks

If in going down through the centuries we run upon a group or groups of people bearing not these distinguishing marks and teaching other things for fundamental doctrines, let us beware.

1. Christ, the author of this religion, organized His followers or disciples into a **Church**. And the disciples were to organize other churches as this religion spread and other disciples were "made." (Ray, Bapt, Succession, Revised Edition, 1st Chap.)

2. This organization or church, according to the Scriptures and according to the practice of the Apostles and early churches, was given two kinds of officers and only two -- pastors and deacons. The pastor was called "Bishop." Both pastor and deacons to be selected by the church and to be servants of the church.

3. The churches in their government and discipline to be entirely separate and independent of each other, Jerusalem to have no authority over Antioch -- nor Antioch over Ephesus; nor Ephesus over Corinth, and so forth. And their government to be congregational, democratic. A government of the people, by the people, and for the people.

4. To the church were given two ordinances and only two, Baptism and the Lord's Supper. These to be perpetual and memorial.

5. Only the **"saved"** were to be received as members of the church (Acts 2:47). These saved ones to be saved by grace alone without any works of the law (Eph, 2:5, 8, 9). These saved ones and they only, to be immersed in the name of the Father, Son and Holy Spirit (Matt. 28:19). And only those thus received and baptized, to partake of the Lord's Supper, and the supper to be celebrated only by the church, in church capacity.

6. The inspired scriptures, and they only, in fact, the New Testament and that only, to be the rule and guide of faith and life, not only for the church as an organization, but for each individual member of that organization.

7. Christ Jesus, the founder of this organization and the savior of its members, to be their only priest and king, their only Lord and Lawgiver, and the only head of the churches. The churches to be executive only in carrying out their Lord's will and completed laws, never legislative, to amend or abrogate old laws or to make new ones.

8. This religion of Christ to be individual, personal, and purely voluntary or through persuasion. No physical or governmental compulsion. A matter of distinct individual and personal choice. "Choose you" is the scriptural injunction. It could be neither accepted nor rejected nor lived by proxy nor under compulsion.

9. Mark well! That neither Christ nor His apostles, ever gave to His followers, what is know today as a denominational name, such as "Catholic," "Lutheran," "Presbyterian," "Episcopal," and so forth -- unless the name given by Christ to John was intended for such, "The Baptist," "John the Baptist" (Matt. 11:11 and 10 or 12 other times.) Christ called the individual follower "disciple." Two or more were called "disciples." The organization of disciples, whether at Jerusalem or Antioch or elsewhere, was called Church. If more than one of these separate organizations were referred to, they were called Churches. The word church in the singular was never used when referring to more than one of these organizations. Nor even when referring to them all.

10. I venture to give one more distinguishing mark. We will call it **Complete separation of Church and State**. No combination, no mixture of this spiritual religion with a temporal power. "Religious Liberty," for everybody.

And now, before proceeding with the history itself, let me call your attention to the following chart

I believe, if you will study carefully this chart, you will better understand the history, and it will greatly aid your memory in retaining what you hear and see.

Remember this chart is supposed to cover a period of two thousand years of religious history.

Notice at both top and bottom of the chart some figures, the same figures at both top and bottom - 100, 200, 300, and so on to 2,000.

They represent the twenty centuries of time--the vertical lines separating the different centuries.

Now notice on the chart, near the bottom; other straight lines, this line running left to right, the long way of the chart.

The lines are about the same distance apart as the vertical lines. But you can't see them all the way. They are covered by a very dark spot, representing in history what is known as the "dark ages." It will be explained later. Between the two lowest lines are the names of countries . . . Italy, Wales, England, Spain, France, and so forth, ending with America. These are names of countries in which much history is made during the period covered by the names themselves. Of course not all the history, some history is made in some of the countries in every period. But some special history is made in these special countries, at these special periods.

Now notice again, near the bottom of the chart, other lines a little higher. They, too, covered in part by the "dark ages," they also are full of names, but not names of countries. They are all "nicknames." Names given to those people by their enemies. "Christians"--that is the first: **"The disciples were called Christians first at Antioch"** (Acts 11:26). This occurred about A.D. 43. Either the pagans or Jews gave them that name in derision. All the other names in that column were given in the same manner -- Montanists, Novationists, Donatists, Paulicians, Albigenses, Waldenses, etc., and Ana-Baptists. All of these will again and again be referred to as the lectures progress.

But look again at the chart. See the red circles. They are scattered nearly all over the chart. They represent churches. Single individual churches in Asia, in Africa, in Europe, in mountains and valleys, and so forth. Their being blood red indicates martyr blood. Christ their founder died on the Cross. All the Apostles save two, John and Judas, suffered martyr deaths. Judas betrayed his Lord and died in a suicide. The Apostle John, according to history, was boiled in a great cauldron of oil.

You will note some circles that are solidly black. They represent churches also. But erring churches. Churches that had gone wrong in life or doctrine. There were numbers of these even before the death of Peter, Paul and John.

Having now about concluded with a general introduction and some very necessary and even vital preliminaries, I come to the regular history:

FIRST PERIOD A.D. 30-500

1. Under the strange but wonderful impulse and leadership of John the Baptist, the eloquent man from the wilderness, and under the loving touch and miracle-working power of the Christ Himself, and the marvelous preaching of the 12 Apostles and their immediate successors, the Christian religion spread mightily during the first 500-year period. However, it left a terribly bloody trail behind it. Judaism and Paganism bitterly contested every forward movement. John the Baptist was the first of the great leaders to give up his life. His head was taken off. Soon after him went the Savior Himself, the founder of this Christian religion. He died on the Cross, the cruel death of the Cross.

2. Following their Savior in rapid succession fell many other martyred heroes: Stephen was stoned, Matthew was slain in Ethiopia, Mark dragged through the streets until dead, Luke hanged, Peter and Simeon were crucified, Andrew tied to a cross, James beheaded, Philip crucified and stoned, Bartholomew flayed alive, Thomas pierced with lances, James, the less, thrown from the temple and beaten to death, Jude shot to death with arrows, Matthias stoned to death and Paul beheaded.

3. More than one hundred years had gone by before all this had happened. This hard persecution by Judaism and Paganism continued for two more centuries. And yet mightily spread the Christian religion. It went into all the Roman Empire, Europe, Asia, Africa, England, Wales, and about everywhere else, where there was any civilization. The churches greatly multiplied and the disciples increased continuously. But some of the churches continued to go into error.

4. The first of these changes from New Testament teachings embraced both policy and doctrine. In the first two centuries the individual churches rapidly multiplied and some of the earlier ones, such as Jerusalem, Antioch, Ephesus, Corinth, etc., grew to be very large; Jerusalem, for instance, had many thousand members (Acts 2:41; 4:4, 5:14), possibly 25,000 or even 50,000 or more. A close student of the book of Acts and Epistles will see that Paul had a mighty task even in his day in keeping some of the churches straight. See Peter's and Paul's prophecies concerning the future (II Pet. 2:12; Acts 20:29-31. See also Rev., second and third chapters).

These great churches necessarily had many preachers or elders (Acts 20:17). Some of the bishops or pastors began to assume authority not given them in the New Testament. They began to claim authority over other and smaller churches. They, with their many elders, began to lord it over God's heritage (III John 9). Here was the beginning of an error which has grown and multiplied into many other seriously hurtful errors. Here was the beginning of different orders in the ministry running up finally to what is practiced now by others as well as Catholics. Here began what resulted in an entire change from the original democratic policy and government of the early churches. This irregularity began in a small way, even before the close of the second century. This was possibly the first serious departure from the New Testament church order.

5. Another vital change which seems from history to have had its beginning before the close of the second century was on the great doctrine of **Salvation** itself. The Jews as well as the Pagans, had for many generations, been trained to lay great stress on **Ceremonials**. They had come to look upon types as anti-types, shadows as real substances, and ceremonials as real saving agencies. How easy to come thus to look upon baptism. They reasoned thus: The Bible has much to say concerning baptism. Much stress is laid upon the ordinance and one's duty concerning it. Surely it must have something to do with one's salvation. So that it was in this period that the idea of **"Baptismal Regeneration"** began to get a fixed hold in some of the churches. (Shackelford, page 57; Camp p. 47; Benedict, p. 286; Mosheim, vol. 1, p. 134; Christian, p. 28.)

6. The next serious error to begin creeping in, and which seems from some historians (not all) to have begun in this same century and which may be said to have been an inevitable consequence of the "baptismal regeneration" idea, was a change in the **subjects of baptism**. Since baptism has been declared to be an agency or means to salvation by some erring churches, then the sooner baptism takes place the better. Hence arose "infant baptism." Prior to this "believers" and "believers" only, were regarded as proper subjects for baptism. "Sprinkling" and "pouring" are not now referred to. These came in much later. For several centuries, infants, like others, were **immersed**. The Greek Catholics (a very large branch of the Catholic church) up to this day, have never changed the original form of baptism. They practice infant baptism but have never done otherwise than immerse the children. (Note -- Some of the church historians put the beginning of infant baptism within this century, but I shall quote a short paragraph from Robinson's Ecclesiastical Researches.)

"During the first three centuries, congregations all over the East subsisted in separate independent bodies, unsupported by government and consequently without any secular power over one another. All this time they were baptized churches, and though all the fathers of the first four ages, down to Jerome (A.D. 370), were of Greece, Syria and Africa, and though they give great numbers of histories of the baptism of adults, yet there is not one of the baptism of a child till the year 370." (Compendium of Baptist History, Shackelford, p. 43; Vedder, p. 50; Christian, p, 31; Orchard, p. 50, etc.)

7. Let it be remembered that changes like these here mentioned were not made in a day, nor even within a year. They came about slowly and never within all the churches. Some of the churches vigorously repudiated them. So much so that in A.D. 251, the loyal churches declared non-fellowship for those churches which accepted and practiced these errors. And thus came about the first real official separation among the churches.

8. Thus it will be noted that during the first three centuries three important and vital changes from the teachings of Christ and His Apostles had their beginnings. And one significant event took place, Note this summary and recapitulation:

> The change from the New Testament idea of bishop and church government. This change grew rapidly, more pronounced, and complete and hurtful.
>
> The change from the New Testament teachings as to Regeneration to "baptismal regeneration."
>
> The change from "believers' baptism" to "infant baptism." (This last, however, did not become general nor even very frequent for more than another century.)

9. "Baptismal regeneration" and "infant baptism." These two errors have, according to the testimony of well-established history, caused the shedding of more Christian blood, as the centuries have gone by, than all other errors combined, or than possibly have all wars, not connected with persecution, if you will leave out the recent "World War." Over 50,000,000

Christians died martyr deaths, mainly because of their rejection of these two errors during the period of the "dark ages" alone -- about twelve or thirteen centuries.

10. Three significant facts, for a large majority of the many churches, are clearly shown by history during these first three centuries.

>The separateness and independence of the Churches.

>The subordinate character of bishops or pastors.

>The baptism of believers only.

I quote now from Mosheim--the greatest of all Lutheran church historians. Vol., 1, pages 71 and 72: "But whoever supposes that the bishops of this golden age of the church correspond with the bishops of the following centuries must blend and confound characters that are very different, for in this century and the next, a bishop had charge of a single church, which might ordinarily be contained in a private house; nor was he its Lord, but was in reality its **minister** or servant. . . All the churches in those primitive times were independent bodies, or none of them subject to the jurisdiction of any other. For though the churches which were founded by the Apostles themselves frequently had the honor shown them to be consulted in doubtful cases, yet they had no judicial authority, no control, no power of giving laws. On the contrary, it is as clear as the noonday that all Christian churches had **equal rights**, and were in all respects on a footing of equality."

11. Up to this period, notwithstanding much and serious persecutions, Christianity has had a marvelous growth. It has covered and even gone beyond the great Roman Empire. Almost, if not all the inhabited world has heard the gospel. And, according to some of the church historians, many of the original churches organized by the Apostles are yet intact, and yet loyal to Apostolic teachings. However, as already shown, a number of very marked and hurtful errors have crept in and gotten a permanent hold among many of the churches. Some have become **very** irregular.

12. Persecutions have become increasingly bitter. Near the beginning of the fourth century comes possibly the first definite government edict of persecution. The wonderful growth of Christianity has alarmed the pagan leaders of the Roman Empire. Hence Galerius, the emperor, sent out a direct edict of more savage persecution. This occurred Feb. 24, 303 A.D. Up to this time Paganism seems to have persecuted without any definite laws to that effect.

13. But this edict failed so utterly in its purpose of stopping the growth of Christianity, that this same emperor, Galerius, just eight years thereafter (A.D. 311) passed another edict recalling the first and actually granting **toleration** -- permission to live the religion of Jesus Christ. This was probably its first favorable law.

14. By the beginning of the year A.D. 313, Christianity has won a mighty victory over paganism. A new emperor has come to the throne of the Roman Empire. He evidently recognized something of the mysterious power of this religion that continued to grow in spite of persecution. History says that this new emperor who was none other than **Constantine** had a wonderful realistic vision. He saw in the skies a fiery red cross and on that cross written in fiery letters these words--"By this thou shalt conquer." He interpreted it to mean that he should become a Christian. And that by giving up paganism and that by attaching the spiritual power of the Christian religion onto the temporal power of the Roman Empire the world could be easily conquered. Thus the Christian religion would in fact become a whole world religion, and the Roman Empire a whole world empire.

15. So under the leadership of Emperor Constantine there comes a truce, a courtship and a proposal of marriage. The Roman Empire through its emperor seeks a marriage with Christianity. Give us your spiritual power and we will give you of our temporal power.

16. To effectually bring about and consummate this unholy union, a council was called. In A. D. 313, a call was made for a coming together of the Christian churches or their representatives . Many but not all came. The alliance was consummated. **A Hierarchy** was formed. In the organization of the **Hierarchy**, Christ was dethroned as head of the **churches** and Emperor Constantine enthroned (only temporarily, however) as head of the **church**.

17. The Hierarchy was the **definite beginning** of a **development** which finally resulted into what is now known as the Catholic, or "universal" church. It might be said that its **indefinite beginnings** were near the close of the second and beginning of the third century, when the new ideas concerning bishops and preacher-church government began to take shape.

18. Let it be definitely remembered that when Constantine made his call for the council, there were very many of the Christians (Baptists) and of the churches, which declined to respond. They wanted no marriage with the state, and no centralized religious government, and no higher ecclesiastical government of any kind, than the individual church. **These Christians (Baptists) nor the churches ever at that time or later, entered the hierarchy of the Catholic denomination.**

19. When this hierarchy was created, Constantine, who was made its head, was not himself at that time a Christian. He had agreed to become one. But as the erring or irregular churches which had gone with him into this organization had come to adopt the error of Baptismal regeneration, a serious question arose in the mind of Constantine, **"If I am saved from my sins by baptism, what is to become of my sins which I may commit after I am baptized?"** He raised a question which has puzzled the world in all succeeding generations. Can baptism wash away yet uncommitted sins? Or, are the sins committed **prior to baptism** washed away by one method (that is, baptism), and the sins committed **subsequent to baptism** washed away by another method?

20. Not being able to settle satisfactorily the many questions thus arising, Constantine finally decided to unite with the Christians, but to postpone his baptism until just preceding his death, so that all his sins might thus be washed away at one time. This course he followed, and hence was not baptized until just preceding his death.

21. Constantine's action in repudiating for the whole Roman Empire, the pagan religion, and accepting Christianity incurred the hot displeasures of the Roman Senate. They repudiated, or, at least opposed his course. And their opposition finally resulted in the removal of the seat of empire from Rome to Byzantium, an old city rebuilt and then renamed Constantinople for Constantine. As a result there came to be two capital cities of the Roman Empire -- Rome and Constantinople. The two rival cities several centuries later became the ruling centers of the divided Catholic church -- Roman and Greek.

22. Up to the organization of the Hierarchy and the uniting of church and state, all the persecution of Christianity has been done either by Judaism or Paganism. Now comes a serious change. Christians (in name) begin to persecute Christians. Constantine, desiring to have all Christians join with him in his new idea of a state religion, and many conscientiously opposing this serious departure from New Testament teachings, he begins using the power of government to compel. Thus begin the days and years and even centuries of a hard and bitter persecution against all those Christians who were loyal to the original Christ and Apostolic teachings.

23. Remember that we are now noting the events occurring between the years A.D. 300 and 500. The Hierarchy organized under the leadership of Constantine, rapidly developed into what is now known as the Catholic church. This newly developing church joined to a temporal government, no longer simply an **executive** to carry out the completed laws of the New Testament, began to be **legislative**, amending or annulling old laws or enacting new ones utterly unknown to the New Testament.

24. One of the first of its legislative enactments, and one of the most subversive in its results, was the **establishing by law of "infant baptism."** By this new law, "Infant Baptism" becomes compulsory. This was done A.D. 416. Infants had been infrequently baptized for probably a century preceding this. Insofar as this newly enacted law became effective, two vital New Testament laws were abrogated -- "Believers Baptism" and "Voluntary personal obedience in Baptism."

25. As an inevitable consequence of this new doctrine and law, these erring churches were soon filled with unconverted members. In fact, it was not very many years until probably a majority of the membership was composed of unconverted material. So the great spiritual affairs of God's great spiritual kingdom were in the hands of an unregenerate temporal power. What may now be expected?

26. Loyal Christians and churches, of course, rejected this new law. "Believers baptism," of course, "New Testament baptism," was the only law for them. They not only refused to baptize their own children, but believing in the baptism of believers only, they refused to accept the baptizing done by and within the churches of this unscriptural organization. If any of the members from the churches of this new organization attempted to join any of the churches which had refused to join in with the new organization, a Christian experience and a rebaptism was demanded.

27. The course followed by the loyal churches soon, of course, incurred the hot displeasure of the state religionists, many, if not most of whom, were not genuine Christians. The name "Christian," however, was from now on denied those loyal churches who refused to accept these new errors. They were robbed of that, and called by many other names, sometimes by one and sometimes by another, "Montanist," Tertullianists," "Novationists," "Paterines," etc., and some at least because of their practice of rebaptizing those who were baptized in infancy, were referred to an "Ana -Baptists."

28. A.D. 426, just ten years after the legal establishment of infant baptism, the awful period known as the "Dark Ages" had its beginning. What a period! How awfully black and bloody! From now on for more than a decade of centuries, the trail of loyal Christianity is largely washed away in its own blood. Note on the chart some of the many different names borne by the persecuted. Sometimes these names are given because of some specially heroic leader and sometimes from other causes, and frequently names for the same people vary in different countries and even in different centuries.

29. It was early in the period of the "dark ages" when real Popery had its definite beginnings. This was by Leo II, A.D. 440

to 461. This, however, was not the first time the title was ever used. This title, similar to the Catholic church itself, was largely a development. The name appears, as first applied to the Bishop of Rome 296-304. It was formally adopted by Siricius, Bishop of Rome 384-398. Then officially adopted by Leo II, 440-461. Then claimed to be universal, 707. Then some centuries later declared by Gregory VII to be the exclusive right of the papacy.

30. Now to sum up the most significant events of this first five-century period:

    The gradual change from a democracy to a preacher-church government.

    The change from salvation by grace to Baptismal Salvation.

    The change from "believers' baptism" to "infant baptism."

    The Hierarchy organized. Marriage of church and state.

    Seat of empire changed to Constantinople.

    Infant baptism established by law and made compulsory.

    Christians begin to persecute Christians.

    The "Dark Ages" begin 426.

    The sword and torch rather than the gospel become the power of God (?) unto salvation.

    All semblance of "Religious liberty" dies and is buried and remains buried for many centuries.

    Loyal New Testament churches, by whatever name called, are hunted and hounded to the utmost limit of the new Cathnlic temporal power. Remnants scattered over the world are finding uncertain hiding places in forests and mountains, valleys, dens and caves of the earth.

SECOND LECTURE—600-1300

1. We closed the first Lecture with the close of the fifth century. And yet a number of things had their beginnings back in those early centuries, which were not even mentioned in the first Lecture. We had just entered the awful period known in the world's history as "The Dark Ages." Dark and bloody and awful in the extreme they were. The persecutions by the established Roman Catholic Church are hard, cruel and perpetual. The war of intended extermination follows persistently and relentlessly into many lands, the fleeing Christians. A "Trail of Blood" is very nearly all that is left anywhere. Especially throughout England, Wales, Africa, Armenia, and Bulgaria. And anywhere else Christians could be found who were trying earnestly to remain strictly loyal to New Testament teaching.

2. We now call attention to these Councils called "Ecumenical," or Empire wide. It is well to remember that all these Councils were professedly based upon, or patterned after the Council held by the Apostles and others at Jerusalem (see Acts 15:1), but probably nothing bearing the same name could have been more unlike. We here and now call attention to only eight, and these were all called by different Emperors, none of them by the Popes. And all these held among the Eastern or Greek churches. Attended, however, somewhat by representatives from the Western Branch or Roman Churches.

3. The first of these Councils was held at Nice or Nicea, in A.D. 325. It was called by Constantine the Great, and was attended by 318 bishops.

The second met at Constantinople, A.D. 381, and was called by Theodosius the Great. There were present 150 bishops. (In the early centuries, bishops simply meant pastors of the individual churches.)

The third was called by Theodosius II, and by Valentian III. This had 250 bishops present. It met at Ephesus, A.D. 431.

The fourth met at Calcedon, A.D. 451, and was called by Emperor Marian; 500 or 600 bishops or Metropolitans

(Metropolitans were City pastors or First Church pastors) were present. During this Council the doctrine of what is now known as **Mariolatry** was promulgated. This means the worship of Mary, the mother of Christ. This new doctrine at first created quite a stir, many seriously objecting. But it finally won out as a permanent doctrine of the Catholic Church.

The fifth of these eight councils was held at Constantinople (which was the second to be held there). This was called by Justinian, A.D. 553, and was attended by 165 bishops. This, seemingly, was called mainly to condemn certain writings.

In the year A.D. 680 the Sixth Council was called. This was also held at Constantinople and was called by Constantine Pegonator, to condemn heresy. During this meeting Pope Honorius by name was deposed and excommunicated. However, at this time infallibility had not yet been declared.

The Seventh Council was called to meet at Nicea A.D. 787. This was the second held at this place. The Empress Irene called this one. Here in this meeting seems to have been the definite starting place, of both "Image Worship" and "Saints Worship." You can thus see that these people were getting more markedly paganized than Christianized.

The last of what were called the "Eastern Councils," those, called by the Emperors, was held in Constantinople, in A.D. 869. This was called by Basilius Maredo. The Catholic Church had gotten into serious trouble. There had arisen a controversy of a very serious nature between the heads of the two branches of Catholicism--the Eastern and Western, Greek and Roman-- Pontius the Greek at Constantinople and Nicholas the 1st at Rome. So serious was their trouble, that they had gone so far as to excommunicate each other. So for a short time Catholicism was entirely without a head. The council was called mainly to settle, if possible, this difficulty. This break in the ranks of Catholicism has never, even to this day, been satisfactorily settled. Since that far away day, all attempts at healing that breach have failed. The Lateran-power since then has been in the ascendancy. Not the Emperors, but the Roman Pontiffs calling all Councils. The later Councils will be referred to later in these lectures.

4. There is one new doctrine to which we have failed to call attention. There are doubtless others but one especially -- and that "Infant Communion." Infants were not only baptized, but received into the church, and being church members, they were supposed to be entitled to the Lord's Supper. How to administer it to them was a problem, but it was solved by soaking the bread in the wine. Thus it was practiced for years. And after awhile another new doctrine was added to this -- it was taught that this was another means of Salvation. As still another new doctrine was later added to these, we will again refer to this a little later in the lectures.

5. During the 5th Century, at the fourth Ecumenical Council, held at Chalcedon, 451, another entirely new doctrine was added to the rapidly growing list -- the doctrine called "Mariolatry," or the worship of Mary, the Mother of Jesus. A new mediator seems to have been felt to be needed. The distance from God to man was too great for just one mediator, even though that was Christ, God's Son, the real God-Man. Mary was thought to be needed as another mediator, and prayers were to be made to Mary. She was to make them to Christ.

6. Two other new doctrines were added to the Catholic faith in the 8th Century. These were promulgated at the Second Council held at Nicea (Nice), the Second Council held there (787). The first of these was called "Image Worship, a direct violation of one of the commands of God.

"Thou shalt not make unto thee any graven image," (Ex. 20:3, 4, 5). Another addition from Paganism. Then followed the "worship of Saints." This doctrine has no encouragement in the Bible. Only one instance of Saint worship is given in the Bible and that is given to show its utter folly -- the dead rich man praying to Abraham, (Luke 16:24-3l). These are some, not all of the many revolutionary changes from New Testament teachings, that came about during this period of Church history.

7. During the period that we are now passing through the persecuted were called by many and varied names. Among them were Donatists, Paterines, Cathari, Paulicians, and Ana Baptists; and a little later, Petro-Brussians, Arnoldists, Henricians, Albigenses, and Waldenses. Sometimes one group of these was the most prominent and sometimes another. But some of them were almost always prominent because of the persistency and terribleness of their persecution.

8. Let it not be thought that all these persecuted ones were always loyal in all respects to New Testament teachings. In the main they were. And some of them, considering their surroundings, were marvelously so. Remember that many of them at that far away, time, had only parts of the New Testament or the Old Testament as to that. The book was not printed. It was written in manuscript on parchment or skins or something of that kind, and was necessarily large and bulky. Few, if any, families or even simple churches had complete copies of the whole Bible. Before the formal close of the Canon (end of fourth century) there were probably very few simple manuscripts of the entire New Testament. Of the one thousand known manuscripts only about 30 copies included all the books.

9. Furthermore, during all the period of the "Dark Ages," and the period of the persecution, strenuous efforts were made to destroy even what Scripture manuscripts the persecuted did possess. Hence in many instances these people had only small parts of the Bible.

10. It is well to note also that in order to prevent the spread of any view of any sort, contrary to those of the Catholics very extreme plans and measures were adopted. First, all writings of any sort, other than those of the Catholics, were gathered and burned. Especially was this true of books. For several centuries these plans and measures were strictly and persistently followed. That is, according to history, the main reason why it is so difficult to secure accurate history. About all persistent writers and preachers also died martyr deaths. This was a desperately bloody period. All of the groups of persistent heretics **(So-called)** by whatever name distinguished, and wherever they had lived, were cruelly persecuted. The Donatists and Paulicians, were prominent among the earlier groups. The Catholics, strange as it may seem, accused all who refused to depart from the faith with them, believe with them--accused them of being **heretics**, and then condemned them as being heretics. Those called Catholics became more thoroughly **paganized** and Judaized than they were Christianized, and were swayed far more by **civil** power, than they were by religious power. They made far more **new laws**, than they observed old ones.

11. The following are a few of the many new variations that came about in New Testament teachings during these centuries. They are probably not always given in the order of their promulgation. In fact it would sometimes be next to impossible to get the exact date of the origin of some of these changes. They have been somewhat like the whole Catholic system. They are growths of development. In the earlier years especially, their doctrines or teachings were subject to constant change -- by addition or subtraction, or substitution or abrogation. The Catholic Church was now no longer, even if it had ever been, a real New Testament Church. It no longer was a purely executive body, to carry out the already made laws of God, but had become actively legislative, making new ones, changing or abrogating old ones at will.

12. One of their new doctrines or declarations about this time was "There is no salvation outside of the Church" -- the Catholic Church, of course, as they declared there was no other -- be a Catholic or be lost. There was no other alternative.

13. The doctrine of **Indulgences** and the Sale of Indulgences was another absolutely new and serious departure from New Testament teachings. But in order to make that new teaching really effective, still another new teaching was imperatively necessary: A very large Credit Account must somehow be established -- a credit account in heaven, but accessible to earth. So the merit of "good works" as a means of Salvation must be taught, and as a means of filling up, putting something in the credit account, from which something could be drawn. The first large sum to go into the account in heaven was of course the work of the Lord Jesus. As He did no evil, none of His good works were needed for Himself, so all His good works could and would of course, go into the credit account. And then in addition to that, all the surplus good works (in addition to what each might need for himself) by the Apostles, and by all good people living thereafter, would be added to that credit account, making it enormously large. And then all this immense sum placed to the credit of the church -- the only church(?)! and permission given to the church to use as needed for some poor sinning mortal, and charging for that credit as much as might be thought wise, for each one needed the heavenly credit. Hence came the Sale of Indulgences. Persons could buy for themselves or their friends, or even dead friends. The prices varied in proportion to the offense committed -- or to be committed. This was sometimes carried to a desperate extreme, as admitted by Catholics themselves. Some histories or Encyclopedias give a list of prices charged on different sins for which Indulgences were sold.

14. Yet another new doctrine was necessary, yea imperative, to make thoroughly effective the last two. That new doctrine is called **Purgatory**, a place of intermediate state between heaven and hell, at which all must stop to be cleansed from all sins less than damning sins. Even the "Saints" must go through purgatory and must remain there until cleansed by fire -- unless they can get help through that credit account, and that they can get only through the prayers or the paying for Indulgences, by those living. Hence the Sale of Indulgences. One departure from New Testament teachings lead inevitably to others.

15. It may be well just here to take time to show the differences between the Roman and Greek Catholics:

> In the Nationalities: The Greeks mainly are Slavs, embracing Greece, Russia, Bulgaria, Serbia, etc., speaking Greek. The Romans are mainly Latins, embracing Italy, France, Spain, South and Central America, Mexico etc.
>
> The Greek Catholics reject sprinkling or pouring for baptism. The Romans use sprinkling entirely, claiming the right to change from the original Bible plan of immersion.
>
> The Greek Catholics continue the practice of Infant Communion. The Romans have abandoned it though once taught it as another means of Salvation.
>
> The Greeks in administering the Lord's Supper give the wine as well as the bread to the laity. The Romans give the bread only to the laity -- the priests drink the wine.

> The Greeks have their priests to marry. The Roman priests are forbidden to marry.
> The Greeks reject the doctrine of Papal "Infallibility," the Romans accept and insist upon that doctrine. The above are at least the main points on which they differ -- otherwise the Greek and Roman Catholic churches, it seems, would stand together.

16. In our lectures we have just about gotten through with the ninth century. We begin now with the tenth. Please note the <u>chart</u>. Just here where the separation has taken place between the Roman and Greek Catholics. You will soon see as the centuries advance, other new laws and doctrines -- and other desperately bitter persecution. (*Schaff, Herzogg, En.*, Vol. 11, page 901.)

17. I again call your attention to those upon whom the hard hand of persecution fell. If fifty million died of persecution during the 1,200 years of what are called the "Dark Ages," as history seems positively to teach -- then they died faster than an average of four million every one hundred years. That seems almost beyond the limit of, human conception. As before mentioned, this iron hand, dripping with martyr blood, fell upon Paulicians, Arnoldists, Henricians, Petro Brussians, Albigenses, Waldenses and Ana-Baptists -- of course much harder upon some than others. But this horrid part of our story we will pass over hurriedly.

18. There came now another rather long period of Ecumenical Councils, of course not continuously or consecutively. There were all through the years many councils that were not Ecumenical, not "Empire Wide." These Councils were largely legislative bodies for the enactment or amendment of some civil or religious (?) laws, all of which, both the legislation and the laws, were directly contrary to the New Testament. Remember these were the acts of an established church -- a church married to a Pagan government. And this church has become far more nearly paganized than the government has become Christianized.

19. When any people discard the New Testament as embracing all necessary laws for a Christian life, whether for the individual

Christian or the whole church, that people has launched upon a limitless ocean. Any erroneous law, (and any law added to the Bible is erroneous) will inevitably and soon demand another, and others will demand yet others, without ever an end. That is why Christ gave His churches and to preachers no legislative powers. And again, and more particularly, that is why the New Testament closes with these significant words, **"For I certify unto every man that heareth the words of this book, if any man shall add unto these things, God shall add unto him the plagues that are written in this book. And if any man shall take away from the words of the book of this prophecy, God shall take away his part out of the book of life, and out of the Holy City, and from the things which are written in the book."** (Rev. 22:18, 19)

> NOTE: We insert here this parenthetical clause, as a warning. Let Baptist Churches beware of even disciplinary and other varieties of resolutions, which they sometimes pass in their conferences, which resolutions might be construed as laws or rules of Church government, The New Testament has all necessary laws and rules.

20. The extreme limit of this little book precludes the possibility of saying much concerning these councils or law-making assemblies, but it is necessary to say some things.

21. The first of these Lateran or Western Councils, those called by the popes, was called by Calixtus II, A.D. 1123. There were present about 300 bishops. At this meeting it was decreed that Roman priests were never to marry. This was called the Celibacy of the priests. We of course do not attempt to give all things done at these meetings.

22. Years later, 1139 A.D., Pope Innocent II, called another of these Councils especially to condemn two groups of very devout Christians, known as Petro-Brussians and Arnoldists.

23. Alexander III called yet another, A.D. 1179, just forty years after the last. In that was condemned what they called the "Errors and Impieties" of the Waldenses and Albigenses.

24. Just 36 years after this last one, another was called by Pope Innocent III. This was held A.D. 1215, and seems to have been the most largely attended of possibly any of these great councils. According to the historical account of this meeting, "there were present 412 bishops, 800 Abbots and priors, Ambassadors from the Byzantine court, and a great number of Princes and Nobles." From the very make-up of this assembly you may know that spiritual matters were at least not alone to be considered.

At that time was promulgated the new doctrine of "Transubstantiation," the intended turning of the bread and wine of the Lord's Supper into the actual and real body and blood of Christ, after a prayer by the priest. This doctrine among others, had much to do with stirring up the leaders of the Reformation a few centuries later. This doctrine of course taught that all those who participated in the supper actually ate of the body and drank of the blood of Christ. Auricular confession -- confessing one's sins into the ear of a priest -- was another new doctrine seemingly having its beginning at this meeting. But probably the most cruel and bloody thing ever brought upon any people in all the world's history was what is known as the "Inquisition," and other similar courts, designed for trying what was called "heresy." The whole world is seemingly filled with books written in condemnation of that extreme cruelty, and yet it was originated and perpetuated by a people claiming to be led and directed by the Lord. For real barbarity there seems to be nothing, absolutely nothing in all history that will surpass it. I would not even attempt to describe it. I will simply refer my readers to some of the many books written on the "Inquisition" and let them read and study for themselves. And yet another thing was done at this same meeting, as if enough had not been done. It was expressly decreed to extirpate all "heresy." What a black page -- yea -- many black pages were written into the world's history by these terrible decrees.

25. In A.D. 1229, just 14 years after the last awful meeting, still another meeting was held. (This seems not to have been ecumenical.) It was called the council at Toulouse. Probably one of the most vital matters in all Catholic history was declared at this meeting. At this it was decreed, the Bible, God's book, should be denied to all laymen, all members of Catholic churches other than priests or higher officials. How strange a law in the face of the plain teaching of the Word, "Search the scriptures; for in them ye think ye have eternal life: and they are they which testify of me." (John 5:39)

26. Yet another Council was called to meet at Lyons. This was called by Pope Innocent IV, in 1245 A.D. This seems to have been mainly for the purpose of excommunicating and deposing Emperor Frederick I of Germany. The Church, the adulterous bride at the marriage with the State in 313 in the days of CONSTANTINE THE Great, has now become the head of the house, and is now dictating politics of State government, and kings and queens are made or unmade at her pleasure.

27. In 1274 A.D. another Council was called to bring about the reuniting of the Roman and Greek branches of the great Catholic Church. This great assembly utterly failed to accomplish its purpose.

THIRD LECTURE--1400-1600

1. These three centuries, fifteenth, sixteenth, and seventeenth, are among the most eventful in all the world's history, and especially is this true in Christian history. There was almost a continual revolution inside the Catholic Church--both Roman and Greek--seeking a Reformation. This awakening of long dormant Conscience and the desire for a genuine reformation really began in the thirteenth century or possibly even a little earlier than that. History certainly seems to indicate it.

2. Let's go back just a little. The Catholic Church by its many departures from New Testament teachings, its many strange and cruel laws, and its desperately low state of morals, and its hands and clothes reeking with the blood of millions of martyrs, has become obnoxious and plainly repulsive to many of its adherents, who are far better than their own system and laws and doctrines and practices. Several of its bravest and best and most spiritual priests and other leaders, one by one, sought most earnestly to reform many of its most objectionable laws and doctrines and get back, at least nearer, to the plain teachings of the New Testament. We give some striking examples. Note, not only how far apart and where the reformatory fires began, but note also the leaders in the reformation. The leaders were, or had been, all Catholic priests or officials of some kind. There was, even yet, a little of good in the much evil. However, **at this time there was probably not one solitary unmarred doctrine of the New Testament retained in its original purity** -- but now note some of the reformers and where they labored.

3. It is well to note, however, that for many centuries prior to this great reformation period, there were a number of noted characters, who rebelled against the awful extremes of the Catholic -- and earnestly sought to remain loyal to the Bible -- but their bloody trail was about all that was left of them. We come now to study for awhile this most noted period -- the "Reformation."

4. From 1320 to 1384 there lived a man in England who attracted world-wide attention. His name was **John Wycliff**. He was the first of the brave fellows who had the courage to attempt a real reformation inside the Catholic Church. He is many times referred to in history as "The Morning Star of the Reformation." He lived an earnest and effective life. It would really require several volumes to contain anything like an adequate history of John Wycliff. He was hated, fearfully hated, by the leaders of the Catholic hierarchy. His life was persistently sought. He finally died of paralysis. But years later, so great was Catholic hatred, his bones were dug and burned, and his ashes scattered upon the waters.

5. Following tolerably close on the heels of Wycliff came **John Huss**, 1373-1415, a distinguished son from far away Bohemia. His soul had felt and responded to the brilliant light of England's "Morning Star." His was a brave and eventful life, but painfully and sadly short. Instead of awakening a responsive chord among his Catholic people in favor of a real reformation, he aroused a fear and hatred and opposition which resulted in his being burned at the stake -- a martyr among his own people. And yet he was seeking their own good. He loved his Lord and he loved his people. However, he was only one of many millions who had thus to die.

6. Next to John Huss of Bohemia, came a wonderful son of Italy, the marvelously eloquent **Savonarola**, 1452-1498. Huss was burned in 1415, Savonarola was born 37 years later. He, like Huss, though a devout Catholic, found the leaders of his people -- the people of Italy -- like those of Bohemia, against all reformation. But he, by his mighty eloquence, succeeded in awakening some conscience and securing a considerable following. But a real reformation in the Hierarchy meant absolute ruin to the higher-ups in that organization. So Savonarola, as well as Huss, must die. HE TOO WAS BURNED AT THE STAKE. Of all the eloquent men of that great period, Savonarola possibly stood head and shoulders above all others. But he was contending against a mighty organization and their existence demanded that they fight the reformation, so Savonarola must die.

7. Of course, in giving the names of the reformers of this period, many names are necessarily to be left out. Only those most frequently referred to in history are mentioned here. Following

Italy's golden tongued orator came a man from Switzerland. **Zwingle** was born before Savonarola died. He lived from 1484 to 1531. The spirit of reformation was beginning now to fill the whole land. Its fires are now breaking out faster and spreading more rapidly and becoming most difficult to control. This one kindled by Zwingle was not yet more than partially smothered before another, more serious than all the rest, had broken out in Germany. Zwingle died in battle.

8. Martin Luther, probably the most noted of all the fifteenth and sixteenth century reformers, lived 1483 to 1546, and as can be seen by the dates, was very nearly an exact contemporary of Zwingle. He was born one year earlier and lived fifteen years later. Far more, probably, than history definitely states, his great predecessors have in great measure made easier his hard way before him. Furthermore, he learned from their hard experience, and then later, and most thoroughly from his own, that a genuine reformation inside the Catholic Church would be an utter impossibility. Too many reform measures would be needed. One would demand another and others demand yet others, and so on and on.

9. So Martin Luther, after many hard fought battles with the leaders of Catholicism, and aided by **Melancthon** and other prominent Germans, became the founder in 1530, or, about then, of an entirely new Christian organization, now known as the Lutheran Church, which very soon became the Church of Germany. This was the first of the new organizations to come directly out of Rome and renounce all allegiance to the Catholic Mother Church (as she is called) and to continue to live thereafter.

10. Skipping now for a little while, the Church of England, which comes next to the Lutheran in its beginnings, we will follow for a little while the Reformation on the Continent. From 1509 to 1564, there lived another of the greatest of the reformers. This was **John Calvin**, a Frenchman, but seeming at the time to be living in Switzerland. He was really a mighty man. He was a contemporary of Martin Luther for 30 years, and was 22 years old when Zwingle died. Calvin is the accredited founder of the Presbyterian church. Some of the historians, however, give that credit to Zwingle, but the strongest evidence seems to favor

Calvin. Unquestionably the work of Zwingle, as well as that of Luther, made much easier the work of Calvin. So in 1541, just eleven years (that seems to be the year), after the founding by Luther of the Lutheran Church, the Presbyterian Church came into existence. It too, as in the case of the Lutherans, was led by a reformed Catholic priest or at least official. These six -- Wycliff, Huss, Savonarola, Zwingle, Luther and Calvin, great leaders in their great battles for reformation, struck Catholicism a staggering blow.

11. In 1560, nineteen years after Calvin's first organization in Geneva, Switzerland, John Knox, a disciple of Calvin, established the first Presbyterian Church in Scotland, and just thirty-two years later, 1592, the Presbyterian became the State Church of Scotland.

12. During all these hard struggles for Reformation, continuous and valuable aid was given to the reformers, by many **Ana-Baptists**, or whatever other name they bore. Hoping for some relief from their own bitter lot, they came out of their hiding places and fought bravely with the reformers, but they were doomed to fearful disappointment. They were from now on to have two additional persecuting enemies. Both the Lutheran and Presbyterian Churches brought out of their Catholic Mother many of her evils, among them her idea of a State Church. They both soon became **Established Churches**. Both were soon in the persecuting business, falling little, if any, short of their Catholic Mother.

Sad and awful was the fate of these long-suffering Ana-Baptists. The world now offered no sure place for hiding. Four hard persecutors were now hot on their trail. Surely theirs was a "Trail of Blood."

13. During the same period, really earlier by several years than the Presbyterians, arose yet another new denomination, not on the continent, but in England. However, this came about not so much by way of reformation (though that evidently made it easier) as by way of a real split or division in the Catholic ranks. More like the division in 869, when Eastern Catholics separated from the Western, and became from that time on, known in history as the Greek and Roman Catholic Churches. This new division came about somewhat in this wise:

England's king, Henry VIII, had married Catherine of Spain, but unfortunately, after some time his somewhat troublesome heart had fallen in love with Anne Boleyn. So he wanted to divorce Catherine and marry Annie. Getting a divorce back then was no easy matter. Only the Pope could grant it, and he in this case, for special reasons, declined to grant it. Henry was in great distress. Being king, he felt he ought to be entitled to follow his own will in the matter. His Prime Minister (at that time Thomas Cromwell) rather made sport of the King. Why do you submit to papal authority on such matters? Henry followed his suggestion, threw off papal authority and made himself head of the Church of England. Thus began the new Church of England. This was consummated in 1534 or 1535. At that time there was no change in doctrine, simply a renunciation of the authority of the Pope. Henry at heart really never became a Protestant. He died in the Catholic faith.

14. But this split did ultimately result in some very considerable change, or reformation, While a reformation **within** the Catholic Church and **under papal authority**, as in the case of Luther and others, was impossible, it became possible after the division. Cranmer, Latimer, Ridley and others led in some marked changes. However, they and many others paid a bloody price for the changes when a few years later, Mary, "Bloody Mary," a daughter of the divorced Catherine, came to the English throne, and carried the new Church back under the papal power. This fearful and terrific reaction ended with the strenuous and bloody five-year reign of Mary. While the heads were going under the bloody axe of Mary, hers went with them. The people had gotten, however, a partial taste of freedom so when Elizabeth, the daughter of Anne Boleyn (for whom Catherine was divorced), became Queen, the Church of England again overthrew papal power and was again re-established.

15. Thus, before the close of the Sixteenth Century, there were five established Churches -- churches backed up by civil governments -- the Roman and Greek Catholics counted as two; then the Church of England; then the Lutheran, or Church of Germany; then the Church of Scotland, now known as the

Presbyterian. All of them were bitter in their hatred and persecution of the people called Ana-Baptists, Waldenses and all other non-established churches, churches which never in any way had been connected with the Catholics. Their great help in the struggle for reformation had been forgotten, or was now wholly ignored. Many more thousands, including both women and children were constantly perishing every day in the yet unending persecutions. The great hope awakened and inspired by the reformation had proven to be a bloody delusion. Remnants now find an uncertain refuge in the friendly Alps and other hiding places over the world.

16. These three new organizations, separating from, or coming out of the Catholics, retained many of their most hurtful errors, some of which are as follows:

>Preacher-church government (differing in form).
>
>Church Establishment (Church and State combination).
>
>Infant BAPTISM
>
>Sprinkling or Pouring for Baptism.
>
>Baptismal Regeneration (some at least, and others, if many of their historians are to be accredited).
>
>Persecuting others (at least for centuries).

17. In the beginning all these established Churches persecuted one another as well as every one else, but at a council held at Augsburg in 1555, a treaty of peace, known as the "Peace of Augsburg" was signed between the "Catholics" on the one hand, and the "Lutherans" on the other, agreeing not to persecute each other. You let us alone, and we will let you alone. For Catholics to fight Lutherans meant war with Germany, and for Lutherans to fight or persecute Catholics meant war with all the countries where Catholicism predominated.

18. But persecutions did not then cease. The hated Ana-Baptists (called Baptists today), in spite of all prior persecutions, and in spite of the awful fact that fifty million had already died martyr deaths, still existed in great numbers. It was during this period that along one single European highway, thirty miles distance, stakes were set up every few feet along this highway, the tops of the stakes sharpened, and on the top of each stake was placed a gory head of a martyred Ana-Baptist. Human imagination can hardly picture a scene so awful! And yet a thing perpetrated, according to reliable history, by a people calling themselves devout followers of the meek and lowly Jesus Christ.

19. Let it be remembered that the Catholics do not regard the **Bible as the sole rule and guide of faith and life**. The claim that it is indeed **unerring**, but that there are two other things just as much so, the "Writings of the Fathers" and the decrees of the Church (Catholic Church) or the declarations of the Infallible Pope.

Hence, there could never be a satisfactory debate between Catholic and Protestant or between Catholic and Baptist, as there could never possibly be a basis of final agreement. The Bible alone can never settle anything so far as the Catholics are concerned.

20. Take as an example the question of "Baptism" and the **final authority** for the act and for the **mode**. They claim that the Bible unquestionably teaches **Baptism** and that it teaches immersion as the **only mode**. But they claim at the same time that their **unerring Church** had the perfect right to **change** the **mode** from **immersion** to **sprinkling** but that no others have the right or authority, none but the infallible papal authority.

21. You will note of course, and possibly be surprised at it, that I am doing in these lectures very little quoting. I am earnestly trying to do a very hard thing, give to the people the main substance of two thousand years of religious history in six hours of time.

22. It is well just here to call attention to facts concerning the Bible during these awful centuries. Remember the Bible was not then in print and there was no paper upon which to have printed even if printing had been invented. Neither was there any paper upon which to write it. Parchment, dressed goat of sheep skins, or papyrus (some kind of wood pulp), this was the stuff used upon which to write. So a book as big as the Bible, all written by hand and with a stylus of some sort, not a pen like we use today, was an enormous thing, probably larger than one man could carry. There were never more than about thirty complete Bibles in all the world. Many parts or books of the Bible like Matthew, Mark, Luke, John, or Acts, or some one of the Epistles, or Revelation or some one book of the Old Testament. One of the most outstanding miracles in the whole world's history -- according to my way of thinking -- is the nearness with which God's people have thought and believed together on the main and vital points of Christianity. Of course God is the only solution. It is now a most glorious fact that we can all and each, now have a full copy of the whole Bible and each in our own native tongue.

23. It is well also for us all to do some serious and special thinking on another vital fact concerning the Bible. It has already been briefly mentioned in the lecture preceding this, but is so very vital that it will probably be wise to refer to it again. It was the action taken by the Catholics at the Council of Toulouse, held in 1229 A. D., when they decided to withhold the Bible, the **Word of God** from the vast majority of all their own people, the "Laymen." I am simply stating here just what they stated in their great Council. But lately in private a Catholic said to me, "Our purpose in that is **to prevent their private interpretation of it."** Isn't it marvelous that God should write a book for the people and then should be unwilling for the people to read it. And yet according to that book the people are to stand or fall in the day of judgment on the teachings of that book. No wonder the declaration in the book -- "Search the Scriptures (the book) for in them ye think ye have eternal life. And they are they which testify of me." Fearful the responsibility assumed by the Catholics!

FOURTH LECTURE -- 17th, 18th, 19th Centuries

1. This lecture begins with the beginning of the Seventeenth Century (A.D. 1601). We have passed very hurriedly over much important Christian history, but necessity his compelled this.

2. This three-century period begins with the rise of an entirely new denomination. It is right to state that some historians give the date of the beginning of the Congregational Church (at first called "Independents") as 1602. However, Schaff-Herzogg, in their Encyclopedia, place its beginning far back in the sixteenth century, making it coeval with the Lutheran and Presbyterian. In the great reformation wave many who went out of the Catholic Church were not satisfied with the extent of the reformation led by Luther and Calvin. They decided to repudiate also the preacher rule and government idea of the churches and return to the New Testament democratic idea as had been held through the fifteen preceding centuries by those who had refused to enter Constantine's hierarchy.

3. The determined contention of this new organization for this particular reform brought down upon its head bitter persecution from Catholic, Lutheran, Presbyterian and Church of England adherents -- all the established churches. However, it retained many other of the Catholic made errors, such for instance as infant baptism, pouring or sprinkling for baptism, and later adopted and practiced to an extreme degree the church and state idea. and, after **refugeeing** to America, themselves, became very bitter persecutors.

4. The name "Independents" or as now called "Congregationalists," is derived from their mode of church government. Some of the distinguishing principles of the English Congregationalists as given in Schaff-Herzogg Encyclopedia are as follows:

> That Jesus Christ is the only head of the church and that the Word of God is its only statue book.

That visible churches are distinct assemblies of Godly men gathered out of the world for purely religious purposes, and not to be confounded with the world.

That these separate churches have full power to choose their own officers and to maintain discipline.

That in respect to their internal management they are each independent of all other churches and equally independent of state control.

5. How markedly different these principles are from Catholicism, or even Lutheranism, or Presbyterianism or the Episcopacy of the Church of England. How markedly similar to the Baptists of today, and of all past ages, and to the original teachings of Christ and His apostles.

6. In 1611, the King James English Version of the Bible appeared. Never was the Bible extensively given to the people before. From the beginning of the general dissemination of the Word of God began the rapid decline of the Papal power, and the first beginnings for at least many centuries, of the idea of "religious liberty."

7. In 1648 came the "Peace of Westphalia." Among other things which resulted from that peace pact was the triple agreement between the great denominations -- Catholic, Lutheran and Presbyterian, no longer to persecute one another. Persecutions among these denominations meant war with governments backing them. However, all other Christians, especially the Ana-Baptists, were to continue to receive from them the same former harsh treatment, persistent persecution.

8. During all the seventeenth century, persecutions for Waldenses, Ana-Baptists, and **Baptists** (in some places the "Ana" was now being left off) continued to be desperately severe; in England by the Church of England, as John Bunyan and many others could testify; in Germany by the Lutherans; in Scotland by the Church of Scotland (Presbyterian); in Italy, in France, and in every other place where the papacy was in power, by the Catholics. There is now no peace anywhere for those who are not in agreement with the state churches, or some one of them.

9. It is a significant fact well established in credible history that even as far back as the fourth century those refusing to go into the Hierarchy, and refusing to accept the baptism or those baptized in infancy, and refusing to accept the doctrine of "Baptismal Regeneration" and demanding rebaptism for all those who came to them from the Hierarchy, were called "Ana-Baptists." No matter what other names they then bore, they were always referred to as "Ana-Baptists." Near the beginning of the sixteenth century, the "Ana" was dropped, and the name shortened to simply "Baptist," and gradually all other names were dropped. Evidently, if Bunyan had lived in an earlier period his followers would have been called "Bunyanites" or "Ana-Baptists." Probably they would have been called by both names as were others preceding him.

10. The name "Baptist" is a "nickname," and was given to them by their enemies (unless the name can be rightfully attributed to them as having been given to them by the Savior Himself, when He referred to John as "The Baptist"). To this day, the name has never been officially adopted by any group of Baptists. The name, however, has become fixed and is willingly accepted and proudly borne. It snugly fits. It was the distinguishing name of the forerunner of Christ, the first to teach the doctrine to which the Baptists now hold.

11. I quote a very significant statement from the Schaff-Herzogg Encyclopedia, under "History of Baptists in Europe," Vol. 1, page 210, "The Baptists appeared first in Switzerland about 1523, where they were persecuted by Zwingle and the Romanists. They are found in the following years, 1525-1530, with large churches fully organized, in Southern Germany, Tyrol and in middle Germany. In all these places persecutions made their lives bitter."

(Note -- that all this is prior to the founding of the Protestant churches--Lutheran, Episcopal, or Presbyterian.)

We continue the quotation: "Moravia promised a home of greater freedom, and thither many Baptists migrated, only to find their hopes deceived. After 1534 they were numerous in Northern Germany, Holland, Belgium, and the Walloon provinces. They increased even during Alva's rule, in the low countries, and developed a wonderful missionary zeal." (Note--"Missionary Zeal." And yet some folks say that the **"Hardshells"** are primitive Baptists.)

Where did these Baptists come from? They did not come out of the Catholics during the Reformation. They had large churches prior to the Reformation.

12. As a matter of considerable interest, note the religious changes in England as the centuries have gone by:

The Gospel was carried to England by the Apostles and it remained Apostolic in its religion until after the organization of the Hierarchy in the beginning of the fourth century, and really for more than another century after that. It then came under the power of the Hierarchy which was rapidly developing into the Catholic Church. It then remained Catholic -- that was the state religion, until the split in 1534-1535, during the reign of Henry VIII. It was then called the Church of England. Eighteen years later, 1553-1558, during the reign of Queen Mary ("Bloody Mary") England was carried back to the Catholics, and a bloody five-years period was this. Then Elizabeth, a half-sister of Mary, the daughter of Anna Boleyn, came to the throne, 1558. The Catholics were again overthrown, and again the Church of England came into power. And thus things remained for almost another century, when the Presbyterian Church came for a short while into the ascendancy, and seemed for a while as if it might become the State Church of England as well as that of Scotland. However, following the time of Oliver Cromwell, the Church of England came back to her own and has remained the established church of England ever since.

13. Note the gradual softening down of religious matters in England from the hard and bitter persecutions of the established church for more than a century.

> The first toleration act came in 1688, one hundred and fifty-four years after the beginning of this church. This act

permitted the worship of all denominations in England except two--the Catholics and the Unitarians.

The second toleration act came in 1778, eighty-nine years still later. This act included in the toleration the Catholics, but still excluded the Unitarians.

The third toleration act came in 1813, thirty-five years later. This included the Unitarians.

In 1828-1829 came what is known as the "Test Act" which gave the "dissenters" (the religionists not in accord with the "Church of England") access to public office and even to Parliament.

In 1836-37 and 1844 came the "Registration" and "Marriage" acts. These two acts made legal baptisms and marriages performed by "dissenters."

The "Reform Bill" came in 1854. This bill opened the doors of Oxford and Cambridge Universities to dissenting students. Up to this time no child of a "dissenter" could enter one of these great institutions.

14. Thus has been the march of progress in England toward "Religious Liberty." But it is probably correct to state that real religious liberty can never come into any country where there is and is to remain an **established church**. At best, it can only be toleration, which is certainly a long way from real religious liberty. As long as one denomination among several in any country is supported by the government to the exclusion of all others this favoritism and support of one, precludes the possibility of absolute religious liberty and equality.

15. Very near the beginning of the eighteenth century there were born in England three boys who were destined to leave upon the world a deep and unfading impression. These boys were **John and Charles Wesley, and George Whitfield.**

John and Charles Wesley were born at Epworth (and here comes a suggestion for the name Epworth League), the former June 28, 1703, and the latter March 29, 1708. George Whitfield was born in Gloucester, December 27, 1714. The story of the lives of these boys cannot be told here, but they are well worth being told, and then retold. These three boys became the fathers and founders of Methodism. They were all three members of the Church of England, and all studying for the ministry; and yet at that time, not one of them converted (which at that time was not unusual among the English clergy. Remember, however, that in those days, the parent frequently, if not usually, decided on the profession or line of the life to be followed by the boy). But these boys were afterwards converted, and genuinely and wonderfully converted.

16. These men seemed to have no desire to be the founders of a new denomination. But they did seem to greatly desire and earnestly strive for a revival of pure religion and a genuine spiritual reformation in the Church of England. This they tried in both England and America. The doors of their own churches were soon closed against them. Their services were frequently held out in the open, or in some private house, or, as especially in the case of Whitfield, in the meeting houses of other denominations. Whitfield's great eloquence attracted markedly great attention everywhere he went.

17. The definite date of the founding of the Methodist Church is hard to be determined. Unquestionably Methodism is older than the Methodist Church. The three young men were called Methodists before they left college. Their first organizations were called "Societies." Their first annual conference in England was held in 1744. The Methodist Episcopal Church was officially and definitely organized in America, in Baltimore in 1784. Their growth has really been marvelous. But, when they came out of the Church of England, or the Episcopal Church, they brought with them a number of the errors of the mother and grandmother churches. For instance, as the Episcopacy, or preacher-church government. On this point they have had many internal wars and divisions, and seem destined to have yet others. Infant Baptism and sprinkling for baptism, etc., but there is one great thing which they have, which they did not bring out with them, a genuine case of spiritual religion.

18. September 12, 1788, there was born in Antrium, Ireland, a child, who was destined in the years to come, to create quite a religious stir in some parts of the world, and to become the founder of a new religious denomination. That child was Alexander Campbell. His father was a Presbyterian minister. The father, Thomas Campbell, came to America in 1807. Alexander, his son, who was then in college, came later. Because of changed views, they left the Presbyterians and organized an independent body, which they called "The Christian Association," known as "The Brush Run Church." In 1811, they adopted immersion as baptism and succeeded in persuading a Baptist preacher to baptize them, but with the distinct understanding that they were not to unite with the Baptist Church. The father, mother, and Alexander were all baptized. In 1813 their independent church united with the Red Stone Baptist Association. Ten years later, because of controversy, they left that association and joined another. Controversies continued to arise, and they left that association. It is fair to say that they had never been Baptists, nor had they so far as any records I have seen, to show, ever claimed to be.

19. It could hardly be fair to Christian history, and especially to Baptist history, to say nothing in these lectures about John Bunyan. In some respects, one of the most celebrated men in English history and even in world history -- John Bunyan, a Baptist preacher -- John Bunyan, twelve years in Bedford jail -- John Bunyan the author while confined in jail, of the most celebrated and most widely circulated book, next to the Bible, in the whole world. "Pilgrim's Progress" -- **John Bunyan**, one of the most notable of all examples of the bitterness of Christian persecution.

And the story of Mary Bunyan, John Bunyan's blind daughter, ought to be in every Sunday School library. For many years it was out of print. I think it is now in print again. I almost defy any man or woman, boy or girl, to read it and keep dry eyes.

20. Another thing about which at least a few words should be said in these lectures in concerning Wales and the Welch Baptists. One of the most thrilling stories in Christian history is the story of the Welch Baptists. The Baptists of the United States owe far most to the Welch Baptists than the most of us are conscious. Some whole Baptist churches, fully organized, have migrated in a body from Wales to the United States. (Orchard, p. 21-23; Ford, chapt. 2.)

21. The story of the beginning of Christian work in Wales is strikingly fascinating and from history it seems to be true. That history begins in the New Testament (Acts 28:30-31; II Tim. 4:21). The story of Claudia and Pudens -- their visit to Rome -- their conversion under Paul's preaching, and carrying the gospel back to Wales, their homeland, is thrillingly interesting. Paul did this preaching in Rome as early as A.D. 63. Soon after that Claudia, Pudens, and others, among them two preachers, carried the same gospel into England and especially into Wales. How mightily the Welch Baptists have helped the Baptists in America can hardly be estimated.

LECTURE FIVE
RELIGION IN THE UNITED STATES

1. Through the Spanish and others of the Latin races, the Catholics as religionists, came to be the first representatives of the Christian religion in South and Central America. But in North America, except Mexico, they have never strongly predominated. In the territory of what is now the United States except in those sections which were once parts of Mexico they have never been strong enough, even during the Colonial period to have their religious views established by law.

2. Beginning with the Colonial period, in the early part of the seventeenth century, the first settlements were established in Virginia, and a little later in that territory now known as the New England States. Religious, or more properly speaking -- irreligious persecutions, in England, and on the continent, were, at least, among the prime causes which led to the first settlement of the first United States Colonies. In some of the groups of immigrants which first came, not including the Jamestown group (1607) and those known as the "Pilgrims" (1620), were two groups, one, at least, called "Puritans" -- these were "Congregationalists." Governor Endicott was in control of their colony. The other group were Presbyterians. Among these two groups, however, were a number of Christians with other views than theirs, also seeking relief from persecution.

"THE TRAIL OF BLOOD IN AMERICA"

3. These refugeeing Congregationalists and Presbyterians established different Colonies and immediately within their respective territories established by law their own peculiar religious views. In other words, "Congregationalism" and "Presbyterianism" were made the legal religious views of their colonies. This to the absolute exclusion of all other religious views. Themselves fleeing the mother country, with the bloody marks of persecution still upon them and seeking a home of freedom and liberty for themselves, immediately upon being established in their own colonies, in the new land and having the authority, they deny religious liberty to others, and practice upon them the same cruel methods of persecution. **Especially did they, so treat the Baptists.**

4. The Southern colonies in Virginia, North and South Carolina were settled mainly by the adherents of the Church of England. The peculiar views of the Church were made the established religion of these colonies. Thus in the new land of America, where many other Congregationalists, Presbyterians and Episcopalians have come seeking the privilege of worshipping God according to the dictates of their own consciences, there were soon set up three established churches. No religious liberty for any except for those who held governmental authority. The Children of Rome are following in the bloody footsteps of their mother. Their own reformation is yet far from complete.

5. With the immigrants to America came many scattering Baptists (by some still called "Ana-Baptists"). There were probably some in every American-bound vessel. They came, however, in comparatively small groups, never in large colonies. They would not have been permitted to come in that way. But they kept coming. Before the colonies are thoroughly established the Baptists are numerous and almost everywhere. But they soon began to feel the heavy hands of the three State churches. For the terrible offenses of "preaching the Gospel" and "refusing to have their children baptized," "opposing infant baptism," and other like conscientious acts on their part, they were arrested, imprisoned, fined, whipped, banished, and their property confiscated, etc. All that here in America. From many sources, I give but a few illustrations.

6. Before the Massachusetts Bay Colony is twenty years old, with the Congregational as the State Church, they passed laws against the Baptists and others. The following is a sample of the laws:

> "It is ordered and agreed, that if any person or persons, within this jurisdiction, shall either openly condemn or oppose the baptizing of infants, or go about secretly to seduce others from the approbation or use thereof, or shall purposely depart the congregation at the ministration of the ordinance . . . after due time and means of conviction --

every such person or persons shall be sentenced to banishment." This law was enacted especially against the Baptists.

7. By the Authorities in this colony, **Roger Williams** and others were banished. Banishment in America in those days was something desperately serious. It meant to go and live among the Indians. In this case Williams was received kindly and for quite a while lived among the Indians, and in after days proved a great blessing to the colony which had banished him. He saved the colony from destruction by this same tribe of Indians, by his earnest entreaties in their behalf. In this way he returned good for evil.

8. Roger Williams, later, together with others, some of whom, at least, had also been banished from that and other of the colonies among whom was **John Clarke**, a Baptist preacher, decided to organize a colony of their own. As yet they had no legal authority from England to do such a thing, but they thought this step wiser under existing conditions than to attempt to live in existing colonies with the awful religious restrictions then upon them. So finding a small section of land as yet unclaimed by any existing colony they proceeded to establish themselves on that section of land now known as Rhode Island. That was in the year 1638, ten years later than the Massachusetts Bay Colony, but it was about 25 years later (1663) before they were able to secure a legal charter.

9. In the year 1651 (?) Roger Williams and John Clarke were sent by. the colony to England to secure, if possible legal permission to establish their colony. When they reached England, Oliver Cromwell was in charge of the government, but for some reason he failed to grant their request. Roger Williams returned home to America. **John Clarke remained in England to continue to press his plea. Year after year went by. Clarke continued to remain. Finally Cromwell lost his position and Charles II sat upon the throne of England. While Charles is regarded in history as one of the bitterest of persecutors of Christians, he finally, in 1663, granted that charter. So Clarke, after 12 long years of waiting returned home with that charter. So in 1663, the Rhode Island colony became a**

real legal institution, and the Baptists could write their own constitution.

10. That Constitution was written. It attracted the attention of the whole wide world. In that Constitution was the world's first declaration of "Religious Liberty."

The battle for absolute religious liberty even in America alone is a great history within itself. For a long time the Baptists seem to have fought that battle entirely alone, but they did not fight it for themselves alone, but for all peoples of every religious faith. Rhode Island, the first Baptist colony, established by a small group of Baptists after 12 years of earnest pleading for permission was the first spot on earth where religious liberty was made the law of the land. The settlement was made in 1638; the colony legally established in 1663.

11. In this colony two Baptist churches were organized even prior to the legal establishment of the colony. As to the exact date of the organization of at least one of these two churches, even the Baptists, according to history, are at disagreement. All seem tn be agreed as to the date of the organization of the one at Providence, by Roger Williams, in 1639. As to the date of the one organized at Newport by John Clarke, all the later testimony seems to give the date at 1638. All the earlier seems to give it later, some years later. The one organized by Roger Williams at Providence seems to have lived but a few months. The other by John Clarke at Newport, is still living. My own opinion as to the date of organization of Newport church, based on all available data, is that **1638** is the correct date. Personally, I am sure this date is correct.

12. As to the persecutions in some of the American colonies, we give a few samples. It is recorded that on one occasion one of John Clarke's members was sick. The family lived just across the Massachusetts Bay Colony line and just inside that colony. John Clarke, himself, and a visiting preacher by the name of Crandall and a layman by the name of Obediah Holmes -- all three went to visit that sick family. While they were holding some kind of a prayer service with that sick family, some officer or officers of the colony came upon them and arrested them and later carried them before the court for trial. It is also stated, that in order to get a more definite charge against them, they were carried into a religious meeting of their church (Congregationalist), their hands being tied (so the record states). The charge against them was "for not taking off their hats in a religious service." They were all tried and convicted. Gov. Endicott was present. In a rage he said to Clarke, while the trial was going on, "You have denied infants baptism" (this was not the charge against them). "You deserve death. I will not have such trash brought into my jurisdiction." The penalty for all was a fine, or be well-whipped. Crandall's fine (a visitor) was five pounds ($25.00), Clarke's fine (the pastor) was twenty pounds ($100.00). Holmes' fine (the records say he had been a Congregationalist and had joined the Baptists) so his fine was thirty pounds ($150.00). Clark's and Crandall's fines were paid by friends. Holmes refused to allow his fine paid, saying he had done no wrong, so was well whipped. The record states that he was "stripped to the waist" and then whipped (with some kind of a special whip) until the blood ran down his body and then his legs until his shoes overflowed. The record goes on to state that his body was so badly gashed and cut that for two weeks he could not lie down, so his body could touch the bed. His sleeping had to be done on his hands or elbows and knees. Of this whipping and other things connected with it I read all records, even Holmes' statement. A thing could hardly have been more brutal. And here in America!

13. Painter, another man, "refused to have his child baptized," and gave as his opinion "that infant baptism was an anti-Christian ordinance." For these offenses he was tied up and whipped. Governor Winthrop tells us that Painter was whipped "for reproaching the Lord's ordinance."

14. In the colony where Presbyterianism was the established religion, dissenters (Baptist and others) seemed to fare no better than in the Massachusetts Bay Colony where Congregationalism was the established religion.

In this colony was a settlement of Baptists. In the whole settlement were only five other families. The Baptists recognized the laws they were under and were, according to the records, obedient to them. This incident occurred: It was decided by authorities of the colony to build a Presbyterian meeting house in that Baptist settlement. The only way to do it seemed by taxation. The Baptists recognized the authority of the Presbyterians to levy this new and extra tax, but they made this plea against the tax at this time -- "We have just started our settlement. Our little cabins have just been built, and little gardens and patches just been opened. Our fields not cleared. We have just been taxed to the limit to build a fort for protection against the Indians. We cannot possibly pay another tax now." This is only the substance of their plea. The tax was levied. It could not possibly be paid at that time. An auction was called. Sales were made. Their cabins and gardens and patches, and even their graveyards, were sold -- not their unopened fields. Property valued at 363 pounds and 5 shillings sold for 35 pounds and 10 shillings. Some of it, at least, was said to have been bought by the preacher who was to preach there. The settlement was said to have been left ruined.

A large book could be filled with oppressive laws. Terrifically burdensome acts of taxation, hard dealing of many sorts, directed mainly against the Baptists. But these lectures cannot enter into these details.

15. In the southern colonies, throughout the Carolinas and especially Virginia, where the Church of England held sway, persecution of Baptists was serious and continuous. Many times their preachers were fined and imprisoned. From the beginning of the colonial period to the opening of the Revolutionary War, more than 100 years, these persecutions of Baptists were persisted in.

16. We give some examples of the hardships of the Baptists in Virginia, and yet strange as it may now seem Virginia was the next place on earth after Rhode Island to adopt religious liberty. But that was more than a century away. But the hardships -- as many as 30 preachers at different times, were put in jail with the only charge against them -- "for preaching the Gospel of the Son of God." James Ireland is a case in point. He was imprisoned. After imprisonment, his enemies tried to blow him up with gunpowder. That having failed, they next tried to smother him to death by burning sulphur under his windows at the jail. Failing also in this, they tried to arrange with a doctor to poison him. All this failed. He continued to preach to his people from the windows. A wall was then built around his jail so the people could not see in nor he see out, but even that difficulty was overcome. The people gathered, a handkerchief was tied to a long stick, and that stuck up above the walls so Ireland could see when they were ready. The preaching continued.

17. Three Baptist preachers (Lewis and Joseph Craig and Aaron Bledsoe) were later arrested on the same charge. One of them, at least, was a blood relative of R. E. B. Baylor, and possibly of one or more other Texas Baptist preachers. These preachers were arraigned for trial. Patrick Henry, hearing of it and though living many miles away and though a Church of England man himself, rode those miles horseback to the trial and volunteered his services in their defense. Great was his defense. I cannot enter into a description of it here. It swept the court. The preachers were freed.

18. Elsewhere than Rhode Island, religious liberty came slowly and by degrees. For example: In Virginia a law was passed permitting one, but only one, Baptist preacher to a county. He was permitted to preach but once in two months. Later this law was modified, permitting him to preach once in each month. But even then, in only one definite place in the county, and only one sermon on that day, and **never** to preach at night. Laws were passed not only in Virginia but in colonies elsewhere **positively forbidding any Mission work.** This was why Judson was the first foreign missijnary -- law forbade. It took a long time and many hard battles, in the Virginia House of Burgesses, to greatly modify these laws.

19. Evidently, one of the greatest obstructions to religious liberty in America, and probably all over the world as to that, was the conviction which had grown into the people throughout the preceding centuries that religion could not possibly live **without governmental support.** That no denomination could prosper solely on voluntary offerings by its adherents. And this was the hard argument to meet when the battle was raging for the disestablishment of the Church of England in Virginia, and also later in Congress when the question of religious liberty was being discussed there. For a long time the Baptists fought the battle almost alone,

20. Rhode Island began her colony in 1638, but it was not legally chartered until 1663. There was the first spot where Religious Liberty was granted. The second place was Virginia in 1786. Congress declared the first amendment to the Constitution to be in force December 15, 1791, which granted religious liberty to all citizens, Baptists are credited with being the leaders in bringing this blessing to the nation.

21. We venture to give one early Congressional incident. The question of whether the United States should have an established church or several established churches, or religious liberty, was being discussed. Several different bills had been offered, one recommending the Church of England as the established church; and another the Congregationalist Church, and yet another the Presbyterian. The Baptists, many of them, though probably none of them members of Congress, were earnestly contending for absolute religious liberty. James Madison (afterwards President) seemingly was their main supporter. Patrick Henry arose and offered a substitute bill for them all, "That **four churches** (or denominations) **instead of one be established**" -- the Church of England, or Episcopal, Congregationalist, Presbyterian, and the Baptist. Finally when each of the others saw that IT could not be made the sole established church, they each agreed to accept Henry's compromise. (This compromise bill stated that each person taxed would have the right to say to which denomination of these four his money should go.) The Baptists continued to fight against it all; that any combination of Church and State was against their fundamental principles, that they could not accept it even if voted. Henry pleaded with them, said he was trying to help them, that they could not live without it, but they still protested. The vote was taken -- it carried nearly unanimously. But the measure had to be voted on three times. The Baptists, led by Madison and possibly others continued to fight. The second vote came. It also carried almost unanimously, swept by Henry's masterful eloquence. But the third vote had yet to be taken. Now God seemingly intervened. Henry was made Governor of Virginia and left Congress. When the third vote came, deprived of Henry's irresistible eloquence, the vote was lost.

Thus the Baptists came near being an established denomination over their own most solemn protest. This is not the only opportunity the Baptists ever had of becoming **established** by law, but is probably the nearest they ever came to it.

22. Not long after this, the Church of England was entirely disestablished in America. No religious denomination was supported by the Central Government (a few separated State governments still had establishment), Church and state, so far as the United States was concerned, were entirely separated. These two, Church and State, elsewhere at least, had for 1,500 years (since 313) been living in unholy wedlock. Religious Liberty was, at least here in the United States, resurrected to die no more, and now gradually but in many places slowly, it is spreading throughout the world.

23. But even in the United States, the Church and State idea died hard. It lingered on in several of the separate States, long after Religious Liberty had been put into the Constitution of the United States. Massachusetts, where the Church and State idea first found a lodging place in America, has, as already stated, finally given it up. It had lived there over two and one-half centuries. Utah is the last lingering spot left to disfigure the face of the first and greatest nation on earth to adopt and cherish "Religious Liberty." Remember there can be no real and absolute Religious liberty in any nation where the Government gives its support to one special religious denomination.

24. Some serious questions have many times been asked concerning the Baptists: Would they, as a denomination, have accepted from any nation or state an offer of "establishment" if such nation or state had freely made them such an offer? And, would they, in case they had accepted such an offer, have become persecutors of others like Catholics or Episcopals, or Lutherans or Presbyterians, or Congregationalists? Probably a little consideration of such questions now would not be amiss. Have the Baptists, as a fact, ever had such an opportunity?

Is it not recorded in history, that on one occasion, the King of the Netherlands (the Netherlands at that time embracing Norway and Sweden, Belgium, Holland, and Denmark) had under serious consideration the question of having an established religion? Their kingdom at that period was surrounded on almost all sides by nations or governments with established religions -- religions supported by the Civil Government.

It is stated that the King of Holland appointed a committee to examine into the claims of all existing churches or denominations to see which had the best claim to be the New Testament Church. The committee reported back that the Baptists were the best representatives of New Testament teachings. Then the King offered to make the Baptist "the established" church or denomination of his kingdom. The Baptists kindly thanked him but declined, stating that it was contrary to their fundamental convictions and principles.

But this was not the only opportunity they ever had of having their denomination the established religion of a people. They certainly had that opportunity when Rhode Island Colony was founded. And to have persecuted others -- that would have been an impossibility if they were to continue being Baptists. They were the original advocates of "Religious Liberty." That really is one of the fundamental articles of their religious faith. They believed in the absolute separation of church and state.

25. So strong has been the Baptist conviction on the question of Church and State combination, that they have invariably declined all offers of help from the State. We give here two instances. One in Texas and the other in Mexico. Long years ago in the days of Baylor University's babyhood, Texas offered to help her. She declined the help though she was in distressing need. The Texas Methodists had a baby school in Texas at the same time. They accepted the State help; that school finally fell into the hands of the State.

The case in Mexico occurred in this wise: W. D. Powell was our missionary to Mexico. By his missionary work he had made a great impression for the Baptists upon Governor Madero of the State of Coahuila. Madero offered a great gift to the Baptists from the State, if the Baptists would establish a good school in the State of Coahuila, Mexico. The matter was submitted by Powell to the Foreign Board. The gift was declined because it was to be from the State. Afterwards Madero gave a good large sum personally. That was accepted and Madero Institute was built and established.

SOME AFTER WORDS

1. During every period of the "Dark Ages" there were in existence many Christians and many separate and independent Churches, some of them dating back to the times of the Apostles, which were never in any way connected with the Catholic Church. They always wholly rejected and repudiated the Catholics and their doctrines. This is a fact clearly demonstrated by credible history.

2. These Christians were the perpetual objects of bitter and relentless persecution. History shows that during the period of the "Dark Ages," about twelve centuries, beginning with A.D. 426, there were about fifty millions of these Christians who died martyr deaths. Very many thousands of others, both preceding and succeeding the "Dark Ages," died under the same hard hand of persecution.

3. These Christians, during these dark days of many centuries, were called by many different names, all given to them by their enemies. These names were sometimes given because of some specially prominent and heroic leader and sometimes from other causes; and sometimes, yea, many times, the same people, holding the same views, were called by different names in different localities. But amid all the many changes of names, there was one special name or rather designation, which clung to at least some of these Christians, throughout all the "Dark Ages," that designation being "Ana-Baptist." This compound word applied as a designation of some certain Christians was first found in history during the third century; and a **suggestive fact** soon after the origin of Infant Baptism, and a more suggestive fact even **prior** to the use of the name **Catholic**. Thus the name "Ana-Baptists" is the oldest **denominational** name in history.

4. A striking peculiarity of these Christians was and continued to be in succeeding centuries: They rejected the man-made doctrine of "Infant Baptism" and demanded rebaptism, even though done by immersion for all those who came to them, having been baptized in infancy. For this peculiarity they were called "Ana-Baptists."

5. This, special designation was applied to many of these Christians who bore other nicknames; especially is this true of the Donatists, Paulicians, Albigenses and Ancient Waldenses and others. In later centuries this designation came to be a regular name, applied to a distinct group. These were simply called "Ana- Baptists" and gradually all other names were dropped. Very early in the sixteenth century, even prior to the origin of the Lutheran Church, the first of all the Protestant Churches, the word "ana" was beginning to be left off, and they were simply called "Baptists."

6. Into the "dark ages" went a group of many churches which were never in any way identified with the Catholics. Out of the "dark ages" came a group of many churches, which had never been in any way identified with the Catholics.

The following are some of the fundamental doctrines to which they held when they went in: And the same are, the fundamental doctrines to which they held when they came out: And the same are the fundamental doctrines to which they now hold.

FUNDAMENTAL DOCTRINES

1. A spiritual Church, Christ its founder, its only head and law giver.

2. Its ordinances, only two, Baptism and the Lord's Supper. They are typical and memorial, not saving.

3. Its officers, only two, bishops or pastors and deacons; they are servants of the church.

4. Its Government, a pure Democracy, and that executive only, never legislative.

5. Its laws and doctrines: The New Testament and that only.

6. Its members. Believers only, they saved by grace, not works, through the regenerating power of the Holy Spirit.

7. Its requirements. Believers on entering the church to be baptized, that by immersion, then obedience and loyalty to all New Testament laws.

8. The various churches -- separate and independent in their execution of laws and discipline and in their responsibilities to God--but cooperative in work.

9. Complete separation of Church and State.

10. Absolute Religious liberty for all.

Partial list of books used in preparing lectures on
"The Trail of Blood"

History of Baptists in Virginia, Semple
Baptist Succession, Ray
Baptists in Alabama, Holcomb
History of the Huguenots, Martin
Fifty Years Among the Baptists, Benedict
Fox's Book of Martyrs
My Church, Moody
The World's Debt to Baptists, Porter
Church Manual, Pendleton
Evils of Infant Baptism, Howell
Reminiscences, Sketches and Addresses, Hutchinson
Short History of the Baptists, Vedder
The Struggle Religious Liberty in Virginia, James
The Genesis of American Anti-Missionism, Carroll
The True Baptist, A. Newton
A Guide to the Study of Church History, McGlothlin
Baptist Principles Reset, Jeter
Virginia Presbyterianism and Religious Liberty in Colonial and Revolutionary Times, Johnson
Presbyterianism 300 Years Ago, Breed
History of the Presbyterian Church of the World, Reed
Catholic Belief, Bruno
Campbellism Examined, Jeter
History of the Baptists in New England, Burrage
History of Redemption, Edwards
Principles and Practices of Baptist Churches, Wayland
History of the Liberty Baptist Association of North Carolina, Sheets
On Baptism, Carson
History and Literature of the Early Churches, Orr
History of Kentucky Baptists, Spencer
Baptist History, Orchard
Baptist Church Perpetuity, Jarrell
Disestablishment, Harwood
Progress of Baptist Principles, Curtis
Story of the Baptists, Cook
Romanism in Its Home, Eager
Americanism Against Catholicism, Grant
The Faith of Our Fathers, Cardinal Gibbons

The Faith of Our Fathers Examined, Stearns
The Story of Baptist Missions, Hervey
Baptism, Conant
Christian "Baptism," Judson
Separation of Church and State in Virginia, Eckenrode
The Progress of Religious Liberty, Schaff
Doctrines and Principles of the M. E. Church
The Churches of the Piedmont, Allix
The History of the Waldenses, Muston
The History of Baptists, Backus
The Ancient Waldenses and Albigenses, Faber
The History of the Waldenses of Italy, Combs
History of the Baptists, Benedict
Baptist Biography, Graham
Early English Baptists, Evans
History of the Welsh Baptists, Davis
Baptist History, Cramp
History of the Baptists, Christian
Short History of the Baptists, Vedder
The Plea for the Cumberland Presbyterian Church, Jones
Religions of the World, Many writers
History of the Reformation in Germany, Ranke
Church History, Kurtz
Constitution of the Presbyterian Church in the USA
Doctrines and Discipline, African M. E. Church, Emory
Church History, Jones
History of the Christian Religion and Church, Neader
Ecclesiastical History, Mosheim
History of the Christian Church, Gregory
History of the Church, Waddington
Handbook of Church History, Green
Manual of Church History, Newman
History of Anti-Pedobaptists, Newman
Catholic Encyclopedia (16 vols.)
The Baptist Encyclopedia, Cathcart
Encyclopedia of Religious Knowledge, Brown
Encyclopedia Britannica
Origin of Disciples, Whittsitt
Encyclopedia of Religious Knowledge, Schaff-Herzogg
Book of Martyrs, Foxe
Baptist History, Schackleford

100	200	300	400	500
IRREGULAR CHURCHES	CHURCH GOVERNMENT CHANGED		CHURCH AND STATE UNITED	LEO II POPERY OFICIALLY ESTABLISHED
		(HIERARCHY)		
JESUS ORGANIZES HIS CHURCH MARK 3:16-18	BAPTISMAL REGENERATION	CONSTANTINE 313		MARIOLOTRY
		INFANT BAPTISM	PERSECUTION ACT 303	INFANT BAPTISM ESTABLISHED BY LAW
		NON FELLOWSHIP DECLARED 251		
			TOLERATION ACT 311	
		MONTANISTS	PURITANS	PATERINS CATHARI
CHRISTIANS	NOVATIONS		ANA	
		PATERINS	DON	A
	ITALY WALES			SPAIN FRANCE
ENGLAND			AFRICA	
100	200	300	400	500

EXPLANATION OF THE CHART
By DR. J. M. CARROLL

ILLUSTRATING the History of the Baptist Churches from the time of their founder, the Lord Jesus Christ, until the 20th Century.

1. The purpose of this book and chart is to show according to History that Baptists have an unbroken line of churches since Christ and have fulfilled His prophecy — "I WILL BUILD MY CHURCH AND THE GATES OF HELL SHALL NOT PREVAIL AGAINST IT." In the irregular churches is clearly seen the growth of Catholicism and Protestantism. Baptists are not Protestants since they did not come out of the Catholic Church.

THE TRAIL OF B[

	600	700	800	900	1000
					INFANT COMMUNION
				DIVISION	GREE
	(C A T H O L I C)			869	
	INDULGENCES	PURGATORY	SAINT AND IMAGE WORSHIP 787		ROMAN
				D A R K	A G E
	P A U L I C I A N				
	B A P T I S T				
	T I S T S WALES	S ARMENIA	ITALY ENGLAND	ARMENIA BULGARIA	F IT
	600	700	800	900	1000

2. The numbers at the top and bottom represent 20 centuries. The first vertical line is A.D. 1, and the second, A.D. 100, and so on.

3. The horizontal lines at the bottom have between them the nicknames given to Baptists during the passing years and ages — Novations, Montanists, Paulicans and Waldenses.

4. THE RED CIRCLES REPRESENT BAPTIST CHURCHES beginning with the first Church at Jerusalem, founded by Christ during His earthly ministry, and out of which came the churches of Judea, Antioch and others. The red indicates they were persecuted. In spite of the bitterest opposition and persecution Baptist Churches are found in every age. The first nickname given them was Christians, the next Ana-Baptists, and so on. You will notice that the dark ages are represented by a dark space. Even

OOD *By* DR. J. M. CARROLL

1100	1200	1300	1400	1500
(CATHOLIC)				
K		1215 DEPOSED FREDERICK	WYCLIFF 1330-1384	1483 SAVONAROLA 1452-1498
TRANSUB- STANTIATION	1123 CELIBACY PETROBR- USIANS & ARNOLDISTS 1139	AURICULAR CONFESSION 1215 INQUISITION 1231		HUSS 1373-1415
(CATHOLIC)				
S		1229 BIBLE FORBIDDEN		ZWI 1484
	ARNOLDISTS	ALBIGENSES		B
(ANA-BAPTISTS)				
RANCE LY	HENRICIANS ENGLAND WALES	W A L D E N GERMANY ITALY	POLAND	ALPS
1100	1200	1300	1400	1500

during this time you will notice a continual line of churches called Ana-Baptists. They were continually and bitterly persecuted even unto death by the Catholics. Near the first of the 16th Century the Ana was dropped and they were simply called Baptists.

5. THE BLACK CIRCLES REPRESENT CHURCHES INTO WHICH ERROR CAME AND ARE THEREFORE CALLED — IRREGULAR CHURCHES. The first error was in church Government — Pastors assumed authority not given them by Christ. Pastors of larger churches claimed authority over other and smaller churches. Thus in the 3rd Century the Roman Hierarchy was established. The Emperor Constantine issued a call in 313 inviting all churches to send representatives to form a council. The red churches — that is Baptist Churches — refused the invitation but the irregular churches responded. The

	1600	1700	1800	1900	2000
TRENT					
1546 LUTHER					
	(1530) (LUTHERAN)				
1509-1564 CALVIN			●	(1810) (CUMBERLAND)	
	(1541) (PRESBYTERIAN)				
1555 AUGSBURG ●	1648 WESTPHALIA		●	(1812) (DISCIPLES)	
	(1602) (CONGREGATIONALIST)				
1531		(CHURCH) (OF) (ENGLAND)			
NGLI 1531 ●	BUNYAN 1628-1688 ●	(1785) (METHODIST)			
		○ ○ ○ ○ ○			
A P T I S T S			● ●	●	
(BAPTISTS) ●●●●●●●●●●●●●●●					
SES					
GERMANY	FRANCE	AMERICA	RUSSIA CUBA		
1600	1700	1800	1900	2000	

Emperor was made the head and thus the group of churches known as irregular churches became the State Church. The Emperor continued to head the churches until Leo II claimed authority as the successor of Peter. Thus is seen how the error in church Government developed into Popery. In the 16th Century the Protestant Churches began to come out of the Roman Catholic Church. They are called Protestants because they protested against the errors of Catholicism.

6. It was in the year 251 that Baptist Churches declared nonfellowship with the irregular churches. They refused to accept Baptism administered in infancy or for Salvation and thus came the oldest nickname — Ana-Baptists which means rebaptizers.

www.ingramcontent.com/pod-product-compliance
Lightning Source LLC
LaVergne TN
LVHW041547080125
800829LV00006B/138

Website:	
Username:	
Password:	
Notes / Security Questions:	

Website:	
Username:	
Password:	
Notes / Security Questions:	

Website:	
Username:	
Password:	
Notes / Security Questions:	

Website:	
Username:	
Password:	
Notes / Security Questions:	

Website:	
Username:	
Password:	
Notes / Security Questions:	

Website:	
Username:	
Password:	
Notes / Security Questions:	

Website:	
Username:	
Password:	
Notes / Security Questions:	

Website:	
Username:	
Password:	
Notes / Security Questions:	

Website:	
Username:	
Password:	
Notes / Security Questions:	

Website:	
Username:	
Password:	
Notes / Security Questions:	

Website:	
Username:	
Password:	
Notes / Security Questions:	

Website:	
Username:	
Password:	
Notes / Security Questions:	

Website:	
Username:	
Password:	
Notes / Security Questions:	

Website:	
Username:	
Password:	
Notes / Security Questions:	

Website:	
Username:	
Password:	
Notes / Security Questions:	

Website:	
Username:	
Password:	
Notes / Security Questions:	

B

Website:	
Username:	
Password:	
Notes / Security Questions:	

Website:	
Username:	
Password:	
Notes / Security Questions:	

Website:	
Username:	
Password:	
Notes / Security Questions:	

Website:	
Username:	
Password:	
Notes / Security Questions:	

Website:	
Username:	
Password:	
Notes / Security Questions:	

Website:	
Username:	
Password:	
Notes / Security Questions:	

Website:	
Username:	
Password:	
Notes / Security Questions:	

Website:	
Username:	
Password:	
Notes / Security Questions:	

B

Website:	
Username:	
Password:	
Notes / Security Questions:	

Website:	
Username:	
Password:	
Notes / Security Questions:	

Website:	
Username:	
Password:	
Notes / Security Questions:	

Website:	
Username:	
Password:	
Notes / Security Questions:	

Website:	
Username:	
Password:	
Notes / Security Questions:	

Website:	
Username:	
Password:	
Notes / Security Questions:	

Website:	
Username:	
Password:	
Notes / Security Questions:	

Website:	
Username:	
Password:	
Notes / Security Questions:	

C

Website:	
Username:	
Password:	
Notes / Security Questions:	

Website:	
Username:	
Password:	
Notes / Security Questions:	

Website:	
Username:	
Password:	
Notes / Security Questions:	

Website:	
Username:	
Password:	
Notes / Security Questions:	

Website:	
Username:	
Password:	
Notes / Security Questions:	

Website:	
Username:	
Password:	
Notes / Security Questions:	

Website:	
Username:	
Password:	
Notes / Security Questions:	

Website:	
Username:	
Password:	
Notes / Security Questions:	

C

Website:	
Username:	
Password:	
Notes / Security Questions:	

Website:	
Username:	
Password:	
Notes / Security Questions:	

Website:	
Username:	
Password:	
Notes / Security Questions:	

Website:	
Username:	
Password:	
Notes / Security Questions:	

D

Website:	
Username:	
Password:	
Notes / Security Questions:	

Website:	
Username:	
Password:	
Notes / Security Questions:	

Website:	
Username:	
Password:	
Notes / Security Questions:	

Website:	
Username:	
Password:	
Notes / Security Questions:	

Website:	
Username:	
Password:	
Notes / Security Questions:	

Website:	
Username:	
Password:	
Notes / Security Questions:	

Website:	
Username:	
Password:	
Notes / Security Questions:	

Website:	
Username:	
Password:	
Notes / Security Questions:	

D

Website:	
Username:	
Password:	
Notes / Security Questions:	

Website:	
Username:	
Password:	
Notes / Security Questions:	

Website:	
Username:	
Password:	
Notes / Security Questions:	

Website:	
Username:	
Password:	
Notes / Security Questions:	

Website:	
Username:	
Password:	
Notes / Security Questions:	

Website:	
Username:	
Password:	
Notes / Security Questions:	

Website:	
Username:	
Password:	
Notes / Security Questions:	

Website:	
Username:	
Password:	
Notes / Security Questions:	

Website:	
Username:	
Password:	
Notes / Security Questions:	

Website:	
Username:	
Password:	
Notes / Security Questions:	

Website:	
Username:	
Password:	
Notes / Security Questions:	

Website:	
Username:	
Password:	
Notes / Security Questions:	

E

Website:	
Username:	
Password:	
Notes / Security Questions:	

Website:	
Username:	
Password:	
Notes / Security Questions:	

Website:	
Username:	
Password:	
Notes / Security Questions:	

Website:	
Username:	
Password:	
Notes / Security Questions:	

Website:	
Username:	
Password:	
Notes / Security Questions:	

Website:	
Username:	
Password:	
Notes / Security Questions:	

Website:	
Username:	
Password:	
Notes / Security Questions:	

Website:	
Username:	
Password:	
Notes / Security Questions:	

Website:	
Username:	
Password:	
Notes / Security Questions:	

Website:	
Username:	
Password:	
Notes / Security Questions:	

Website:	
Username:	
Password:	
Notes / Security Questions:	

Website:	
Username:	
Password:	
Notes / Security Questions:	

F

Website:	
Username:	
Password:	
Notes / Security Questions:	

Website:	
Username:	
Password:	
Notes / Security Questions:	

Website:	
Username:	
Password:	
Notes / Security Questions:	

Website:	
Username:	
Password:	
Notes / Security Questions:	

Website:	
Username:	
Password:	
Notes / Security Questions:	

Website:	
Username:	
Password:	
Notes / Security Questions:	

Website:	
Username:	
Password:	
Notes / Security Questions:	

Website:	
Username:	
Password:	
Notes / Security Questions:	

Website:	
Username:	
Password:	
Notes / Security Questions:	

Website:	
Username:	
Password:	
Notes / Security Questions:	

Website:	
Username:	
Password:	
Notes / Security Questions:	

Website:	
Username:	
Password:	
Notes / Security Questions:	

F

Website:	
Username:	
Password:	
Notes / Security Questions:	

Website:	
Username:	
Password:	
Notes / Security Questions:	

Website:	
Username:	
Password:	
Notes / Security Questions:	

Website:	
Username:	
Password:	
Notes / Security Questions:	

Website:	
Username:	
Password:	
Notes / Security Questions:	

Website:	
Username:	
Password:	
Notes / Security Questions:	

Website:	
Username:	
Password:	
Notes / Security Questions:	

Website:	
Username:	
Password:	
Notes / Security Questions:	

Website:	
Username:	
Password:	
Notes / Security Questions:	

Website:	
Username:	
Password:	
Notes / Security Questions:	

Website:	
Username:	
Password:	
Notes / Security Questions:	

Website:	
Username:	
Password:	
Notes / Security Questions:	

Website:	
Username:	
Password:	
Notes / Security Questions:	

Website:	
Username:	
Password:	
Notes / Security Questions:	

Website:	
Username:	
Password:	
Notes / Security Questions:	

Website:	
Username:	
Password:	
Notes / Security Questions:	

Website:	
Username:	
Password:	
Notes / Security Questions:	

Website:	
Username:	
Password:	
Notes / Security Questions:	

Website:	
Username:	
Password:	
Notes / Security Questions:	

Website:	
Username:	
Password:	
Notes / Security Questions:	

Website:	
Username:	
Password:	
Notes / Security Questions:	

Website:	
Username:	
Password:	
Notes / Security Questions:	

Website:	
Username:	
Password:	
Notes / Security Questions:	

Website:	
Username:	
Password:	
Notes / Security Questions:	

Website:	
Username:	
Password:	
Notes / Security Questions:	

Website:	
Username:	
Password:	
Notes / Security Questions:	

Website:	
Username:	
Password:	
Notes / Security Questions:	

Website:	
Username:	
Password:	
Notes / Security Questions:	

Website:	
Username:	
Password:	
Notes / Security Questions:	

Website:	
Username:	
Password:	
Notes / Security Questions:	

Website:	
Username:	
Password:	
Notes / Security Questions:	

Website:	
Username:	
Password:	
Notes / Security Questions:	

Website:	
Username:	
Password:	
Notes / Security Questions:	

Website:	
Username:	
Password:	
Notes / Security Questions:	

Website:	
Username:	
Password:	
Notes / Security Questions:	

Website:	
Username:	
Password:	
Notes / Security Questions:	

Website:	
Username:	
Password:	
Notes / Security Questions:	

Website:	
Username:	
Password:	
Notes / Security Questions:	

Website:	
Username:	
Password:	
Notes / Security Questions:	

Website:	
Username:	
Password:	
Notes / Security Questions:	

Website:	
Username:	
Password:	
Notes / Security Questions:	

Website:	
Username:	
Password:	
Notes / Security Questions:	

Website:	
Username:	
Password:	
Notes / Security Questions:	

Website:	
Username:	
Password:	
Notes / Security Questions:	

I

Website:	
Username:	
Password:	
Notes / Security Questions:	

Website:	
Username:	
Password:	
Notes / Security Questions:	

Website:	
Username:	
Password:	
Notes / Security Questions:	

Website:	
Username:	
Password:	
Notes / Security Questions:	

I

Website:	
Username:	
Password:	
Notes / Security Questions:	

Website:	
Username:	
Password:	
Notes / Security Questions:	

Website:	
Username:	
Password:	
Notes / Security Questions:	

Website:	
Username:	
Password:	
Notes / Security Questions:	

Website:	
Username:	
Password:	
Notes / Security Questions:	

Website:	
Username:	
Password:	
Notes / Security Questions:	

Website:	
Username:	
Password:	
Notes / Security Questions:	

Website:	
Username:	
Password:	
Notes / Security Questions:	

J

Website:	
Username:	
Password:	
Notes / Security Questions:	

Website:	
Username:	
Password:	
Notes / Security Questions:	

Website:	
Username:	
Password:	
Notes / Security Questions:	

Website:	
Username:	
Password:	
Notes / Security Questions:	

Website:	
Username:	
Password:	
Notes / Security Questions:	

Website:	
Username:	
Password:	
Notes / Security Questions:	

Website:	
Username:	
Password:	
Notes / Security Questions:	

Website:	
Username:	
Password:	
Notes / Security Questions:	

Website:	
Username:	
Password:	
Notes / Security Questions:	

Website:	
Username:	
Password:	
Notes / Security Questions:	

Website:	
Username:	
Password:	
Notes / Security Questions:	

Website:	
Username:	
Password:	
Notes / Security Questions:	

Website:	
Username:	
Password:	
Notes / Security Questions:	

Website:	
Username:	
Password:	
Notes / Security Questions:	

Website:	
Username:	
Password:	
Notes / Security Questions:	

Website:	
Username:	
Password:	
Notes / Security Questions:	

Website:	
Username:	
Password:	
Notes / Security Questions:	

Website:	
Username:	
Password:	
Notes / Security Questions:	

Website:	
Username:	
Password:	
Notes / Security Questions:	

Website:	
Username:	
Password:	
Notes / Security Questions:	

Website:	
Username:	
Password:	
Notes / Security Questions:	

Website:	
Username:	
Password:	
Notes / Security Questions:	

Website:	
Username:	
Password:	
Notes / Security Questions:	

Website:	
Username:	
Password:	
Notes / Security Questions:	

Website:	
Username:	
Password:	
Notes / Security Questions:	

Website:	
Username:	
Password:	
Notes / Security Questions:	

Website:	
Username:	
Password:	
Notes / Security Questions:	

Website:	
Username:	
Password:	
Notes / Security Questions:	

L

Website:	
Username:	
Password:	
Notes / Security Questions:	

Website:	
Username:	
Password:	
Notes / Security Questions:	

Website:	
Username:	
Password:	
Notes / Security Questions:	

Website:	
Username:	
Password:	
Notes / Security Questions:	

L

Website:	
Username:	
Password:	
Notes / Security Questions:	

Website:	
Username:	
Password:	
Notes / Security Questions:	

Website:	
Username:	
Password:	
Notes / Security Questions:	

Website:	
Username:	
Password:	
Notes / Security Questions:	

L

Website:	
Username:	
Password:	
Notes / Security Questions:	

Website:	
Username:	
Password:	
Notes / Security Questions:	

Website:	
Username:	
Password:	
Notes / Security Questions:	

Website:	
Username:	
Password:	
Notes / Security Questions:	

L

Website:	
Username:	
Password:	
Notes / Security Questions:	

Website:	
Username:	
Password:	
Notes / Security Questions:	

Website:	
Username:	
Password:	
Notes / Security Questions:	

Website:	
Username:	
Password:	
Notes / Security Questions:	

Website:	
Username:	
Password:	
Notes / Security Questions:	

Website:	
Username:	
Password:	
Notes / Security Questions:	

Website:	
Username:	
Password:	
Notes / Security Questions:	

Website:	
Username:	
Password:	
Notes / Security Questions:	

Website:	
Username:	
Password:	
Notes / Security Questions:	

Website:	
Username:	
Password:	
Notes / Security Questions:	

Website:	
Username:	
Password:	
Notes / Security Questions:	

Website:	
Username:	
Password:	
Notes / Security Questions:	

Website:	
Username:	
Password:	
Notes / Security Questions:	

Website:	
Username:	
Password:	
Notes / Security Questions:	

Website:	
Username:	
Password:	
Notes / Security Questions:	

Website:	
Username:	
Password:	
Notes / Security Questions:	

Website:	
Username:	
Password:	
Notes / Security Questions:	

Website:	
Username:	
Password:	
Notes / Security Questions:	

Website:	
Username:	
Password:	
Notes / Security Questions:	

Website:	
Username:	
Password:	
Notes / Security Questions:	

Website:	
Username:	
Password:	
Notes / Security Questions:	

Website:	
Username:	
Password:	
Notes / Security Questions:	

Website:	
Username:	
Password:	
Notes / Security Questions:	

Website:	
Username:	
Password:	
Notes / Security Questions:	

Website:	
Username:	
Password:	
Notes / Security Questions:	

Website:	
Username:	
Password:	
Notes / Security Questions:	

Website:	
Username:	
Password:	
Notes / Security Questions:	

Website:	
Username:	
Password:	
Notes / Security Questions:	

Website:	
Username:	
Password:	
Notes / Security Questions:	

Website:	
Username:	
Password:	
Notes / Security Questions:	

Website:	
Username:	
Password:	
Notes / Security Questions:	

Website:	
Username:	
Password:	
Notes / Security Questions:	

Website:	
Username:	
Password:	
Notes / Security Questions:	

Website:	
Username:	
Password:	
Notes / Security Questions:	

Website:	
Username:	
Password:	
Notes / Security Questions:	

Website:	
Username:	
Password:	
Notes / Security Questions:	

O

Website:	
Username:	
Password:	
Notes / Security Questions:	

Website:	
Username:	
Password:	
Notes / Security Questions:	

Website:	
Username:	
Password:	
Notes / Security Questions:	

Website:	
Username:	
Password:	
Notes / Security Questions:	

O

Website:	
Username:	
Password:	
Notes / Security Questions:	

Website:	
Username:	
Password:	
Notes / Security Questions:	

Website:	
Username:	
Password:	
Notes / Security Questions:	

Website:	
Username:	
Password:	
Notes / Security Questions:	

O

Website:	
Username:	
Password:	
Notes / Security Questions:	

Website:	
Username:	
Password:	
Notes / Security Questions:	

Website:	
Username:	
Password:	
Notes / Security Questions:	

Website:	
Username:	
Password:	
Notes / Security Questions:	

O

Website:	
Username:	
Password:	
Notes / Security Questions:	

Website:	
Username:	
Password:	
Notes / Security Questions:	

Website:	
Username:	
Password:	
Notes / Security Questions:	

Website:	
Username:	
Password:	
Notes / Security Questions:	

Website:	
Username:	
Password:	
Notes / Security Questions:	

Website:	
Username:	
Password:	
Notes / Security Questions:	

Website:	
Username:	
Password:	
Notes / Security Questions:	

Website:	
Username:	
Password:	
Notes / Security Questions:	

Website:	
Username:	
Password:	
Notes / Security Questions:	

Website:	
Username:	
Password:	
Notes / Security Questions:	

Website:	
Username:	
Password:	
Notes / Security Questions:	

Website:	
Username:	
Password:	
Notes / Security Questions:	

Website:	
Username:	
Password:	
Notes / Security Questions:	

Website:	
Username:	
Password:	
Notes / Security Questions:	

Website:	
Username:	
Password:	
Notes / Security Questions:	

Website:	
Username:	
Password:	
Notes / Security Questions:	

Website:	
Username:	
Password:	
Notes / Security Questions:	

Website:	
Username:	
Password:	
Notes / Security Questions:	

Website:	
Username:	
Password:	
Notes / Security Questions:	

Website:	
Username:	
Password:	
Notes / Security Questions:	

Q

Website:	
Username:	
Password:	
Notes / Security Questions:	

Website:	
Username:	
Password:	
Notes / Security Questions:	

Website:	
Username:	
Password:	
Notes / Security Questions:	

Website:	
Username:	
Password:	
Notes / Security Questions:	

Q

Website:	
Username:	
Password:	
Notes / Security Questions:	

Website:	
Username:	
Password:	
Notes / Security Questions:	

Website:	
Username:	
Password:	
Notes / Security Questions:	

Website:	
Username:	
Password:	
Notes / Security Questions:	

Q

Website:	
Username:	
Password:	
Notes / Security Questions:	

Website:	
Username:	
Password:	
Notes / Security Questions:	

Website:	
Username:	
Password:	
Notes / Security Questions:	

Website:	
Username:	
Password:	
Notes / Security Questions:	

Q

Website:	
Username:	
Password:	
Notes / Security Questions:	

Website:	
Username:	
Password:	
Notes / Security Questions:	

Website:	
Username:	
Password:	
Notes / Security Questions:	

Website:	
Username:	
Password:	
Notes / Security Questions:	

Website:	
Username:	
Password:	
Notes / Security Questions:	

Website:	
Username:	
Password:	
Notes / Security Questions:	

Website:	
Username:	
Password:	
Notes / Security Questions:	

Website:	
Username:	
Password:	
Notes / Security Questions:	

Website:	
Username:	
Password:	
Notes / Security Questions:	

Website:	
Username:	
Password:	
Notes / Security Questions:	

Website:	
Username:	
Password:	
Notes / Security Questions:	

Website:	
Username:	
Password:	
Notes / Security Questions:	

Website:	
Username:	
Password:	
Notes / Security Questions:	

Website:	
Username:	
Password:	
Notes / Security Questions:	

Website:	
Username:	
Password:	
Notes / Security Questions:	

Website:	
Username:	
Password:	
Notes / Security Questions:	

Website:	
Username:	
Password:	
Notes / Security Questions:	

Website:	
Username:	
Password:	
Notes / Security Questions:	

Website:	
Username:	
Password:	
Notes / Security Questions:	

Website:	
Username:	
Password:	
Notes / Security Questions:	

S

Website:	
Username:	
Password:	
Notes / Security Questions:	

Website:	
Username:	
Password:	
Notes / Security Questions:	

Website:	
Username:	
Password:	
Notes / Security Questions:	

Website:	
Username:	
Password:	
Notes / Security Questions:	

S

Website:	
Username:	
Password:	
Notes / Security Questions:	

Website:	
Username:	
Password:	
Notes / Security Questions:	

Website:	
Username:	
Password:	
Notes / Security Questions:	

Website:	
Username:	
Password:	
Notes / Security Questions:	

S

Website:	
Username:	
Password:	
Notes / Security Questions:	

Website:	
Username:	
Password:	
Notes / Security Questions:	

Website:	
Username:	
Password:	
Notes / Security Questions:	

Website:	
Username:	
Password:	
Notes / Security Questions:	

S

Website:	
Username:	
Password:	
Notes / Security Questions:	

Website:	
Username:	
Password:	
Notes / Security Questions:	

Website:	
Username:	
Password:	
Notes / Security Questions:	

Website:	
Username:	
Password:	
Notes / Security Questions:	

Website:	
Username:	
Password:	
Notes / Security Questions:	

Website:	
Username:	
Password:	
Notes / Security Questions:	

Website:	
Username:	
Password:	
Notes / Security Questions:	

Website:	
Username:	
Password:	
Notes / Security Questions:	

Website:	
Username:	
Password:	
Notes / Security Questions:	

Website:	
Username:	
Password:	
Notes / Security Questions:	

Website:	
Username:	
Password:	
Notes / Security Questions:	

Website:	
Username:	
Password:	
Notes / Security Questions:	

Website:	
Username:	
Password:	
Notes / Security Questions:	

Website:	
Username:	
Password:	
Notes / Security Questions:	

Website:	
Username:	
Password:	
Notes / Security Questions:	

Website:	
Username:	
Password:	
Notes / Security Questions:	

Website:	
Username:	
Password:	
Notes / Security Questions:	

Website:	
Username:	
Password:	
Notes / Security Questions:	

Website:	
Username:	
Password:	
Notes / Security Questions:	

Website:	
Username:	
Password:	
Notes / Security Questions:	

Website:	
Username:	
Password:	
Notes / Security Questions:	

Website:	
Username:	
Password:	
Notes / Security Questions:	

Website:	
Username:	
Password:	
Notes / Security Questions:	

Website:	
Username:	
Password:	
Notes / Security Questions:	

Website:	
Username:	
Password:	
Notes / Security Questions:	

Website:	
Username:	
Password:	
Notes / Security Questions:	

Website:	
Username:	
Password:	
Notes / Security Questions:	

Website:	
Username:	
Password:	
Notes / Security Questions:	

Website:	
Username:	
Password:	
Notes / Security Questions:	

Website:	
Username:	
Password:	
Notes / Security Questions:	

Website:	
Username:	
Password:	
Notes / Security Questions:	

Website:	
Username:	
Password:	
Notes / Security Questions:	

Website:	
Username:	
Password:	
Notes / Security Questions:	

Website:	
Username:	
Password:	
Notes / Security Questions:	

Website:	
Username:	
Password:	
Notes / Security Questions:	

Website:	
Username:	
Password:	
Notes / Security Questions:	

Website:	
Username:	
Password:	
Notes / Security Questions:	

Website:	
Username:	
Password:	
Notes / Security Questions:	

Website:	
Username:	
Password:	
Notes / Security Questions:	

Website:	
Username:	
Password:	
Notes / Security Questions:	

Website:	
Username:	
Password:	
Notes / Security Questions:	

Website:	
Username:	
Password:	
Notes / Security Questions:	

Website:	
Username:	
Password:	
Notes / Security Questions:	

Website:	
Username:	
Password:	
Notes / Security Questions:	

Website:	
Username:	
Password:	
Notes / Security Questions:	

Website:	
Username:	
Password:	
Notes / Security Questions:	

Website:	
Username:	
Password:	
Notes / Security Questions:	

Website:	
Username:	
Password:	
Notes / Security Questions:	

Website:	
Username:	
Password:	
Notes / Security Questions:	

Website:	
Username:	
Password:	
Notes / Security Questions:	

Website:	
Username:	
Password:	
Notes / Security Questions:	

Website:	
Username:	
Password:	
Notes / Security Questions:	

Website:	
Username:	
Password:	
Notes / Security Questions:	

Website:	
Username:	
Password:	
Notes / Security Questions:	

Website:	
Username:	
Password:	
Notes / Security Questions:	

Website:	
Username:	
Password:	
Notes / Security Questions:	

Website:	
Username:	
Password:	
Notes / Security Questions:	

Website:	
Username:	
Password:	
Notes / Security Questions:	

Website:	
Username:	
Password:	
Notes / Security Questions:	

Website:	
Username:	
Password:	
Notes / Security Questions:	

Website:	
Username:	
Password:	
Notes / Security Questions:	

Website:	
Username:	
Password:	
Notes / Security Questions:	

Website:	
Username:	
Password:	
Notes / Security Questions:	

Website:	
Username:	
Password:	
Notes / Security Questions:	

Website:	
Username:	
Password:	
Notes / Security Questions:	

Website:	
Username:	
Password:	
Notes / Security Questions:	

Website:	
Username:	
Password:	
Notes / Security Questions:	

Website:	
Username:	
Password:	
Notes / Security Questions:	

Website:	
Username:	
Password:	
Notes / Security Questions:	

Website:	
Username:	
Password:	
Notes / Security Questions:	

Website:	
Username:	
Password:	
Notes / Security Questions:	

Website:	
Username:	
Password:	
Notes / Security Questions:	

Website:	
Username:	
Password:	
Notes / Security Questions:	

Website:	
Username:	
Password:	
Notes / Security Questions:	

Website:	
Username:	
Password:	
Notes / Security Questions:	

Website:	
Username:	
Password:	
Notes / Security Questions:	

Website:	
Username:	
Password:	
Notes / Security Questions:	

Website:	
Username:	
Password:	
Notes / Security Questions:	

Website:	
Username:	
Password:	
Notes / Security Questions:	

Website:	
Username:	
Password:	
Notes / Security Questions:	

Website:	
Username:	
Password:	
Notes / Security Questions:	

Website:	
Username:	
Password:	
Notes / Security Questions:	

Website:	
Username:	
Password:	
Notes / Security Questions:	

Website:	
Username:	
Password:	
Notes / Security Questions:	

Website:	
Username:	
Password:	
Notes / Security Questions:	

Website:	
Username:	
Password:	
Notes / Security Questions:	

Website:	
Username:	
Password:	
Notes / Security Questions:	

Website:	
Username:	
Password:	
Notes / Security Questions:	

Website:	
Username:	
Password:	
Notes / Security Questions:	

Website:	
Username:	
Password:	
Notes / Security Questions:	

Website:	
Username:	
Password:	
Notes / Security Questions:	

Website:	
Username:	
Password:	
Notes / Security Questions:	

Website:	
Username:	
Password:	
Notes / Security Questions:	

Website:	
Username:	
Password:	
Notes / Security Questions:	

Website:	
Username:	
Password:	
Notes / Security Questions:	

Website:	
Username:	
Password:	
Notes / Security Questions:	

Website:	
Username:	
Password:	
Notes / Security Questions:	

Website:	
Username:	
Password:	
Notes / Security Questions:	

Website:	
Username:	
Password:	
Notes / Security Questions:	

Website:	
Username:	
Password:	
Notes / Security Questions:	

Z

Website:	
Username:	
Password:	
Notes / Security Questions:	

Website:	
Username:	
Password:	
Notes / Security Questions:	

Website:	
Username:	
Password:	
Notes / Security Questions:	

Website:	
Username:	
Password:	
Notes / Security Questions:	

Z

Website:	
Username:	
Password:	
Notes / Security Questions:	

Website:	
Username:	
Password:	
Notes / Security Questions:	

Website:	
Username:	
Password:	
Notes / Security Questions:	

Website:	
Username:	
Password:	
Notes / Security Questions:	

Z

Website:	
Username:	
Password:	
Notes / Security Questions:	

Website:	
Username:	
Password:	
Notes / Security Questions:	

Website:	
Username:	
Password:	
Notes / Security Questions:	

Website:	
Username:	
Password:	
Notes / Security Questions:	

Z

Website:	
Username:	
Password:	
Notes / Security Questions:	

Website:	
Username:	
Password:	
Notes / Security Questions:	

Website:	
Username:	
Password:	
Notes / Security Questions:	

Website:	
Username:	
Password:	
Notes / Security Questions:	

www.ingramcontent.com/pod-product-compliance
Lightning Source LLC
Chambersburg PA
CBHW052200261224
19554CB00010B/690